His Story, My Story, Our Story

Praise for *His Story, My Story, Our Story*

"*His Story, My Story, Our Story* is an insightful read regarding the ties that bind a Marine Corps family, and the stresses placed upon those ties. From combat tours, change of station moves, and the memories that often haunt combat veterans, Brian Ahearn lays bare the good, bad, and ugly of being the son of a Marine. Through his eyes, from childhood, to becoming a father himself, we read of hurt, empathy, forgiveness, and reconciliation. This is why "Thank you for your service" means so much to Vietnam veterans and their families, for although the families don't wear the Eagle, Globe, and Anchor, they sacrifice and serve our country, as well."

—**Robert J. Sutter,** (former Captain USMC)
Author of *ODD MAN OUT*

"My father-in-law served in the Marine Corp as a tank commander in Vietnam – an experience that would impact his personal and professional relationships until his passing in 2008. Brian's thoughtful presentation of the experiences our veterans had defending our country and then the impact that the post-traumatic stress disorder (PTSD) had on shaping their interpersonal relationships afterwards should give every reader pause to reflect on the true cost that has been paid by these warriors. "Semper Fi" is more than just a slogan – it is a promise paid in the blood, sweat and tears of anyone who has earned the title of Marine."

—**John Fear,** Owner Premier Business Consulting

"Brian Ahearn and I were close friends for nearly 40 years until the time of his passing. During our friendship we had many conversations about business, fatherhood, life, and eventually his experience with the Vietnam War. Now his son, Brian, authors penetrating stories of the broken lives, the love lost between fathers and sons, and tenderly discovered in life and time. A resolving account of finding his father's love again beautifully written with truth, honor, and forgiveness by the hand of the last son."

—**G. James Caldwell**

"Father and son relationships can be complex and challenging even under the best of circumstances however, even more difficult as the result of a father experiencing his own trauma and relationship experiences. *His Story, My Story, Our Story: Eternal Lessons about Fatherhood, Sacrifice and Service* is an unabated story of a father and son relationship that seeks understanding and shows the power of forgiveness and the special bond between father and son. As a Marine, the dynamics of the stress of combat are difficult to explain especially to our children. Brian tells the story of his relationship between he and his father that sheds light on the importance of understanding and the ability to forgive in order to preserve the relationship. The insight of a combat Marine and a son over a lifetime, Brian shines a light on his personal experiences that are often painful however, never gives up on understanding his father and more importantly, loving and respecting him above all! A great read for sons and fathers alike!"

—**Colonel M.G. McCoy,** USMC retired

"As a combat veteran, Brian's book made me take a step back and reevaluate the relationships and interactions I have with my family members. Although my wars were separated from Captain Ahearn's by many years, there are similarities that are relevant for today's war veterans in helping them come to grips with their individual demons. *His Story, My Story, Our Story* also provides information to help family members better understand the various issues their loved ones are struggling with when returning from combat. Brian even goes so far as to offer a variety of resources for you or someone you love. Any veteran would be well served to read Brian's book and share it with their family and friends."

—**Gregg A. Sturdevant,** Major General, United States Marine Corps (Retired)

"In this deeply personal account, written by the son of a U.S. Combat Marine, readers are invited on an intimate journey into the challenges, lasting impact, and unwavering resilience experienced while growing up with a father battling combat PTSD. A captivating blend of biography, human interest, and psychology, Brian's vulnerability draws you in, offering laughter, amazement, and profound self-discovery. As a retired USAF Special Operator, I found *His Story, My Story, Our Story* to be a mirror reflecting my own experiences and a window into the lives of those around me. Brian's story is a compelling exploration of human connection, resilience, and the enduring strength that resides within us all."

—**Anthony Tormey,** USAF, Retired, Speaker, Coach, and Founder of Leader Development Institute

"Brian's book caused a lot of personal reflection on how I approach my family relationships and with others. *His Story, My Story, Our Story* showed me that I wasn't so alone when I came home from Afghanistan. There are more similarities between Captain Brian Ahearn and myself than I care to admit. This turned out to be one of the most personally challenging books I've read. It's pushed me to work on myself and realize that I'm a constant work in progress."

—**Dan Bokros,** former Marine

"For me, *His Story, My Story, Our Story* painted an honest picture of life – not a life or lives. War is not for the faint of heart and often only survived by those of us chosen by the father, to carry out his will and his next mission for us. I believe those of us who get to come home, come home with the continued sense of service, protecting life in honor of those who couldn't. It's a heavy burden but one carried with pride. That pride can be misunderstood, and that pride can produce its own unintended burdens on those we love most to carry. Those we would lay our lives down for the easiest, to save them from the pains of war. That is life though, it's complicated by war and pride but also wrapped in love. Love for brothers, love for our fathers, and love for the sons that will carry our banner into the future generations."

—**Sgt. Nick Blankenship,** USMC

"This great book is about expectations – expectations of self, expectations of family and the expectations of being a Marine in the United States Marine Corps. It's also a book about being on the other side of expectations poorly expressed. This is a story of faith and determination – a determination to be one's own person and live according to a healthy level of integrity and passion. A great read for a Marine, for the families of Marines, and for men and women who have struck out on their own determined to do it better."

—**Bill Walton,** proud son of a Marine

"Brian has penned an excellent and reflective book about his dad in a way that touches the heart as well as educates the reader on the life of a United States Marine. Like Brian, my dad, served as a junior officer in the U.S. Marine Corps for 20 years, so his depiction of Captain Ahearn resonated with me as I read *His Story, My Story, Our Story: Eternal Lessons of Fatherhood, Sacrifice, and Service.* In Section 1, the author shares his own perspectives about his dad that are meaningful and profound. In Section 2, the author uses his dad's words to help the reader to understand his motives, actions, and goals. I highly recommend Brian's book as a way to learn, grow, and appreciate the father-son relationship in our times."

—**Kevin Wayne Johnson,** son of a Marine, CEO, The Johnson Leadership Group

"Brian's book, *His Story, My Story, Our Story*, is a great depiction of how everyone in the family truly deploys. It connects the effects of combat veterans returning home by giving three unique points of views; the child, the wife, and the veteran himself. Brian's book helps military families understand the new dynamic they are facing as a family."

—**Edwin Medina,** U.S. Army, Iraq War Veteran

"Have you ever picked up a book and been so strongly impacted that you didn't want to put it down? Not just because the story is authentic, but because it relates to you personally, and the lives of your loved ones, touching generations. Brian's book, *His Story, My Story, Our Story*, packs an emotionally powerful punch…but not at the gut level. At the heart level. I felt, I lived Brian's journey as a child, a young man, and a married man through the complicated and meaningful relationship with his father. As a veteran myself, and the grandson of a WWII veteran, Brian's book wasn't simply a powerful story; it was insight into the unspoken burdens my grandfather, Bernard, faced and never spoke about. It took a significant toll on my grandfather's health. Yet, the legacy that I carry with me to this day is that of Bernard's bravery, hard work ethic, loyalty, and sense of duty. Just like Brian – and those who have loved ones that are serving and have served – what remains often for the children of a veteran is a mix of gratefulness for an incredible heritage and a life full of painful moments. Brian's book will encourage conversations, compassion, and perhaps forgiveness within those who have not been quite able to identify why their veterans think, act, and feel like they do at times. Brian's book is a source of healing, insight, and hope. I highly recommend it."

—**John Hanson,** U.S. Army veteran

His Story, My Story, Our Story

Eternal Lessons of Fatherhood, Sacrifice, and Service

Brian Ahearn, CPCU, CMCT

NEW YORK

LONDON • NASHVILLE • MELBOURNE • VANCOUVER

His Story, My Story, Our Story
Eternal Lessons of Fatherhood, Sacrifice, and Service

Published in New York, New York, by Morgan James Publishing. Morgan James is a trademark of Morgan James, LLC. www.MorganJamesPublishing.com

Proudly distributed by Publishers Group West®

Scripture quotations taken from the (NASB®) New American Standard Bible®, Copyright © 1960, 1971, 1977, 1995, 2020 by The Lockman Foundation. Used by permission. All rights reserved. lockman.org

The ESV Global Study Bible®, ESV® Bible, Copyright © 2012 by Crossway. All rights reserved.

Chicago. Gibran, Kahlil. 2020. The Prophet. Alma Classics Evergreens. Richmond, England: Alma Classics.

Morgan James BOGO™

A **FREE** ebook edition is available for you or a friend with the purchase of this print book.

CLEARLY SIGN YOUR NAME ABOVE

Instructions to claim your free ebook edition:
1. Visit MorganJamesBOGO.com
2. Sign your name CLEARLY in the space above
3. Complete the form and submit a photo of this entire page
4. You or your friend can download the ebook to your preferred device

ISBN 9781636983288 paperback
ISBN 9781636983295 ebook
Library of Congress Control Number:
2023946217

Cover & Interior Design by:
Christopher Kirk
www.GFSstudio.com

Morgan James PUBLISHING Builds with... **Habitat for Humanity** Peninsula and Greater Williamsburg

Morgan James is a proud partner of Habitat for Humanity Peninsula and Greater Williamsburg. Partners in building since 2006.

Get involved today! Visit: www.morgan-james-publishing.com/giving-back

Table of Contents

Acknowledgments

As you might imagine, writing this book elicited a wide range of emotions within me. There were some painful memories but many more good ones. On the whole, I've led a wonderful life because of family, friends, the experiences I've had, and my faith. While some aspects of growing up in my father's shadow were difficult, as I reflected on it while writing this book, I know I'm a better man, husband, father, and friend as a result of what I learned from him.

A book like this isn't the endeavor of one person. Far from it! I leaned on many people for feedback and insights, so I'd like to acknowledge them.

First is my wife, **Jane Ahearn**. She listened to the book many times and asked insightful questions to help me think more deeply. She was supportive during the toughest times with Dad and always challenges me to be better. She loved Dad so I'm glad she had a hand in developing this book.

Jo Ahearn who was married to my father for 38 years. I'm sure some parts of the book were difficult for her to read. Nonetheless, she supported the effort because, like my father, she loves the Marines and knows it will help many young men and their families.

My sister **Carey Crabbs**. We grew up in the same household but have many different memories. When she told me she enjoyed understanding my perspective on our family history it meant a lot.

General Charlie Wilhelm for his foreword. When I read it for the first time my thought was, *"Dang, he should have written the book!"* As you would expect from a retired Marine general, his writing was crisp and to the point.

Jim Caldwell, a longtime family friend, and very close friend to Dad, read my initial manuscript. He challenged my thinking in many areas, including the original book title. He liked the first draft but felt something was missing that could make it much better. I was encouraged by that and hope I hit the mark with the final version.

Kevin Ahearn and **Rory Ahearn**, my father's two remaining siblings. Each read the book and shared family insights that added to my understanding of the Ahearn clan and my father.

Anthony Tormey, a retired Air Force Pararescue (PJ). We've known each other for decades and Anthony is an *"iron sharpens iron"* friend. His detailed comments, questions, and insights made a difference.

Friends and family who took a look and offered thoughts include **Mark Blackburn, Coach Todd Alles (retired Navy),**

Eric Holden, Loring "Pud" Mellien, Karen Walch, KC Jensen, John Petrucci, Barbara Grassey, and Kate Trosky.

Nancy Edwards edited this manuscript as well as my first three books. I'm a better writer because of Nancy, and her edits always take my books up several notches for readers.

Les Hughes, a developmental editor, who helped rearrange several sections, asked insightful questions, and shared ideas that improved the manuscript immensely.

The Marines who read the book and shared thoughts. More than the feedback, I appreciated how many opened up to me about their Marine Corps experiences. Thank you, Robert Sutter, Dan Bokros, and Mike McCoy.

My mother Ann Strausburg. While she did not read the manuscript, she was on my mind as I wrote. I have more appreciation for how difficult it must have been for her to have been married to my father. She persevered under very difficult circumstances, raising my sister and me as a single parent for a good bit of their tumultuous marriage. Carey and I are better people because of her love and guidance.

Foreword

"The Marines I have seen around the world
have the cleanest bodies, the filthiest minds,
the highest morale, and the lowest morals
of any group of animals I have ever seen.
Thank God for the United States Marine Corps!"
—Eleanor Roosevelt

With his Irish good looks and razor-sharp wit, Brian Ahearn, Captain, U.S.M.C., stood out in a crowd. He was the kind of man who, though you knew him only briefly, you would remember clearly more than a half-century later.

When his son, also named Brian, contacted me and asked if I would write the Foreword to this book, I consented. While reading the manuscript, I realized that there was another very different side to the Marine Officer with whom I served in Vietnam. There are words that need to be spoken and lines that need to be read. This short book draws back the curtains on a man's life, revealing both his vices and virtues.

This is a work in two parts by two authors. The first part is about a man and a Marine, and what it's like to be the son of that man and Marine. This is revealed through the eyes of his son. Therein lies its value to those who serve today and attempt to balance the fulfillment of their duties and obligations, both as Marines and as fathers.

The second part is Captain Brian Ahearn's reflections on his service in the Marine Corps and his experiences as an infantry officer in the Republic of Vietnam. Marines who read this book will immediately realize that while many things have changed in the Corps, most have not. Like all worthy institutions, the Marine Corps has evolved. Eleanor Roosevelt's observations about clean bodies, filthy minds, high morale, and low morals is only partially correct now. The bodies remain clean and morale is high, but morals and minds have been upgraded.

Vietnam is no longer the nation's longest war. Its longevity has been surpassed by the decades-long conflicts in the Middle East. While weapons, missions, and the ways they are carried out have changed, the people have not. The courage and selfless devotion to duty Brian Ahearn recalled from his time in Vietnam have been replicated in Iraq and Afghanistan. The words engraved on the Marine Corps War Memorial, *"Uncommon Valor was a Common Virtue,"* are not, and have not been, bounded by time or geography.

One point, easily missed, that strikes home and is the unifying theme for this book is the statement in Captain Ahearn's obituary, *"Brian IS a Captain in the Marine Corps."* His son dutifully captured the essence of being a Marine. It is a commitment that ignores the boundaries of time and earthly existence. Whether you are a Marine or not, there is much to be learned from these pages about fatherhood, sacrifice, and service.

—Charles E. Wilhelm, General (retired, four stars), United States Marine Corps

Author's Note:

My dad thought the world of General Wilhelm. To help you appreciate the special bond that Marines have with one another, and to help you understand the level of respect my father had for this man, I wanted to include the following remarks about him in my dad's own words.

"One of my platoon commanders was Charlie Wilhelm. Since we were in the rear, Charlie asked if he could go into Danang. Rather unusual for an officer, so I asked why. Charlie responded that a nurse he had met in Washington had herself transferred to Danang Naval Hospital! I said that any woman who came that far deserved to see her Marine. So off Charlie went."

Twenty–six years later, my father wrote:

"While watching news about the first war in Iraq, I saw that the Commanding General of the 1stMarDiv was Charles Wilhelm. I wrote a letter asking if he was the same Charlie from Danang who went to see his nurse friend. I soon received a reply that in fact he was that person and had been married to the nurse for 20+ years."

Finally, in 1999 my father wrote this entry in his journal:

"An article in The Ledger (Lakeland) stated that the commencement address speaker at Florida Southern was to be LtGen. Charles Wilhelm, who had recently been appointed as head of the SouthCom, General Wesley Clark's old billet. The same Charlie and, ironically, a graduate of Florida Southern. We got to talk for a while. It was great to reminisce.

Charlie stayed in the Corps and eventually became the second Marine officer to reach the rank of General (four stars) without being Commandant. Charlie was given this rank when he took command of General Clark's Southern Command."

My dad always said the world of the Marines was a small world. That's true. Their world is not only small, but also surrounded by a bubble that's very hard to penetrate from the outside.

The fact that Dad reached back out to the General after all those years, and that General Wilhelm responded, is a testimony to the galvanized bond between Marines. Their exchange, so natural, as though no time had passed since they served together, can't be completely understood by civilians such as myself. Dad explained the bond between Marines in this way:

"I still find Marine friendships the most rewarding of any, even if they were not from Vietnam. There is an invisible bond that joins us forever. If a Marine has a need, others will step in to help. It must be a carryover from being so close in such terrible times."

Preface

"Let's run with endurance the race
that is set before us."
—Hebrews 12:1 (NASB®)

This book is dedicated to two groups of people. First are the men and women of The United States Marine Corps who lay everything on the line to serve our country. Not second, but right alongside them, the book is dedicated to their families who love them, support them, and quite often have to put up with them. I wrote the book from the perspective of the father-son relationship because that's my experience. I don't know what it's like to be parented by a woman who is serving or has served in The Corps, nor do I know what it's like to be a woman whose father served. Nonetheless, I hope the book helps with those relationships too.

I believe most boys who live with their fathers want to respect them. I respected and looked up to my dad, until I didn't. My father, Brian F.X. Ahearn, Captain, United States Marine Corps, and I had a rough go of it for a number of years, but we ended up in a good place at the time of his passing in September 2020. Above all else, my father was most proud of being a Marine. He identified as a Marine before his roles as a son, a brother, a husband, a father, or anything else. Being part of The Corps was truly who he was at his core. I'm fortunate that later in life he opened up to me. Eventually he wrote about his time in the Marines and his experience in Vietnam. His writings helped me understand him and empathize with him far more than I would have on my own.

Let me briefly foreshadow the book. For those who are Marines, you will appreciate the section entitled *Being A Marine*. In that section, my father wrote about why he joined The Corps, his unforgettable experiences at boot camp, his time in Officer Candidate School, his combat tour in Vietnam, and his return home. Before you get to that section, you'll learn about our family history and my experience growing up in my father's shadow. In the final section, I share some scenes from my father's funeral service, including my eulogy.

The book is intended to honor my father, but it's raw in many places. That's intentional. I didn't sugarcoat the contents. The facts and statements I share are truthful. Admittedly, my perspective as a son, especially when I was a kid, was different from the perspective of my father and other members of the family. Others would relay events differently. I'm okay with that. My goal was to paint an accurate picture of our relationships, with all the complexities, and the lessons I learned as a result. Perhaps my experience can help you in your journey as well.

My father and I shared a lot of things, but not the one thing he cherished most—The Corps. I'm certain that's a major reason my father and I never completely understood one another. But that's only part of our story.

This is a story of hope, forgiveness, and redemption, but our journey often took us through what some call a tunnel of chaos. Your family's story may be mild compared to our journey, or your experience could be much worse. That doesn't matter. What does matter is that you understand you can't always control events, and you certainly can't control other people. You did not decide to be born or adopted into your family. I believe God made that decision.

You do have control over how you respond to events and what you do with those experiences as you move forward. I hope you find some gold nuggets in the insights I share that can help you along the way.

Please keep this in mind as you read the not so flattering accounts—*it's not how we start the race we call "life", but how we finish.* We're all works in progress, and I hope you'll see my father was a different man by the end of his life.

If this book helps one Marine have a better relationship with his or her family, it will be worth the time and effort to write it. I hope Marine family members will read it too, so they get a fresh perspective of the Marine in their lives. That's important because relationships are a two-way street. To repair relationships and rebuild them takes intentional effort from everyone involved.

Admitting mistakes and seeking forgiveness is the most powerful way to restore a relationship. But it takes two to tango. If someone says, *"I'm sorry,"* the relationship isn't *fully* restored until another says, *"And I forgive you."*

The only person you can change is you. While your actions can influence another person, it's still up to them to change. Having said that, your actions can help or hinder another's progress towards positive change. Knowing this, and that relationships take time and effort on the part of both parties, forgiveness is essential. Sometimes little acts can indicate a move to the middle which, if reciprocated, begin to bring people together with or without uttering, *"I forgive you."*

Because my dad is a Marine—it's never *"was a Marine"*, not even in death—I know he would be proud of this book and the journey it represents. He would have done *anything* to help a fellow Marine or a Marine's family. After all, he risked his life in battle for his brothers in arms so why wouldn't he take this next step? That's Semper Fi. Always Faithful. I believe with all my heart my father finds joy knowing he continues to help his brothers and sisters in The Corps well beyond his time on Earth.

As I wrote this book, I decided to also dedicate it to our daughter Abigail. Abigail, your name means source of joy, and you certainly have been that to me and your mother! Our joyful anticipation of your birth and our time raising you, helped your mom and me rethink many aspects of our lives, our marriage, and our success as parents. Your presence also helped us deal with family issues in ways we wouldn't have otherwise.

As I've reflected on our family history and my childhood, I've determined to stop passing along the negative aspects of our family history and instead, to instill the best parts of who we are. While we were far from perfect parents, Abigail, I hope you and your children benefit from the efforts your mom and I put forth.

An Unfinished and Unread Letter

"There is an appointed time for everything.
And there is a time for every matter under heaven:
A time to give birth and a time to die,
a time to kill and a time to heal,
a time to weep and a time to laugh,
a time to be silent and a time to speak,
a time to love and a time to hate,
a time for war and a time for peace."
—Ecclesiastes 3:1–8 (NASB® edited)

D ad,
I've been reading a book that's forced me to think about you a lot. I decided to write because whenever I talk to Jane or Abigail about it, I just cry. I'm sure I'll shed tears as I write this. If I ramble or jump around, it's because there are a lot of thoughts to process.

The book I'm referring to is *The Body Keeps the Score: Brain, Mind and Body in the Healing of Trauma* by Bessel van der Kolk. Early on the author wrote a lot about PTSD and Vietnam vets. Many aspects he wrote about, and that vets share, I *"knew"* intellectually, but I couldn't identify with experientially. Somehow as I read this special book, the information dropped from my head to my heart. I know that because as I lay in bed the other day thinking about it, I cried for quite some time.

As a kid, I obviously had no idea what you went through during Vietnam. I just saw you as my dad, someone who fought over there. From my earliest memories I knew you were tough because my whole life I never saw you back down from anyone over anything. Sometimes the issues were not a big deal, at least in my mind, but you would not back down if you believed you were in the right. I think I inherited that from you—do the right thing because it's the right thing to do. Frankly, it's why I never dabbled in recreational drugs. It was so deeply set in my mind that it was wrong. Believe me, most of my friends dabbled, but I never was tempted to give into *"peer pressure"* because my compass was set on true north.

I think most boys look up to their fathers and seek their approval. From what I know about you and your father, I think that was the case for you. I remember when you told me that you overheard your father tell a coworker you would last only six months at Fairfield because of your poor academic performance at Iona. You said that comment motivated you to make the Dean's List routinely during college.

For you to win your dad's approval was probably made more difficult by his addiction to alcohol. His mind was altered over time, and rational thinking became more challenging as he aged.

Something I've noticed about the Ahearn family is our pride. Despite the successes you had, it was probably never within your dad to admit you'd done things he never did, maybe never could have. That's sad because I believe we should want our children to do better and be more than we are as parents. That's how the world can continually become a better place. I know Jane and I believe the world is a better place since Abigail came into it. She possesses the best traits from both of us and very few of the crappy parts.

I see that Ahearn pride within me; that is, the belief that if I apply myself to something I can be better than anyone else.

—Unfinished and Unread, August 6, 2020

Section 1:
A Son's Perspective

The Marine's Family

"Nothing I have ever done,
or ever will do, can compare
with serving in combat in
The United States Marine Corps."
—Brian F.X. Ahearn, Captain, U.S.M.C.

September 14, 2020

Friday, September 11, 2020, I'm scrolling through my Facebook feed, and I see Dad's picture. He didn't post it. He rarely ever posted anything. It wasn't that he didn't have the ability to write, and write well. He wrote lots of editorials for local newspapers, but Facebook wasn't his thing. The picture I saw on that day was from Jo's timeline. Jo was his wife, my stepmom, and September 11th was their 38th wedding anniversary. As I looked at the picture, I thought to myself, "Wow, Dad looks good! He looks as though he's lost a little weight, and he looks really happy."

Dad on his 38th wedding anniversary

A few days later, Monday, September 14th, I was a guest on a podcast. The podcast host and I decided to record the episode first thing in the morning so we could jump into the rest of our day and workweek. When I finished recording, I checked my phone and noticed a call from Jo. I thought that was strange because Jo almost never called me. She called my wife, Jane, all the time. They were the planners when it came to holidays, vacations, visits, etc. They would usually check with me and Dad for the okay, but they did all the heavy lifting.

Jo's and Jane's relationship is a lot deeper than two people planning events together. They're like two peas in a pod. The similarities are uncanny. Their first names start with J, they married men named Brian Ahearn, they love golf, they're passionate about their faith, and they share the same birthday (May 14). And that's the short list. They couldn't be more like sisters, even if they had the same mother!

Jo's voicemail simply said, "*Brian, this is Jo. Would you please call me as soon as you can? Thank you. Bye.*" I called immediately, and she told me Dad passed away that morning. While I don't recall her exact words because I was in a state of shock, she said he did his normal routine of getting up by six a.m. to walk their Golden Lab, Bella. Jo walked by him when he was in his office and commented that he was back quickly from their walk. He said he hurried back because he needed to use the restroom. Moments later she heard him yell, "*Jo!*" She rushed into his office and saw he'd fallen over in his chair. It was a heart attack. Despite her efforts, and the efforts of the paramedics, he passed away at age 79. He'd had a heart procedure in February of that year and seemed to be doing better than ever. He even commented on how he didn't get out of breath so easily anymore. Regarding the procedure, he emailed me and my sister Carey on January 6, 2020:

> "It is easier for me to email a note than text. As you may know, I have had health problems for the last three+ years, starting in Ohio in 2016. Probably the climate. At the start of 2019 I became short of breath sometimes with minor exertion. Initially, they said it could be emphysema, COPD, or allergies, but never tied it down until I had a series of lung function tests and heart tests. The tests point to

a heart problem. The latest echocardiograms indicate that the problem comes from a damaged valve-not really bad, but it should be replaced. Given my young age, they recommend a catheterization procedure vs open heart surgery. No specific date as I have to have a few more tests and a special consultation. Ironic—the diagnosis comes 54 years to the day when I stepped out of a chopper south of Danang and was blown sky high by a mortar round. It probably means I have another 54 years."

We joked quite a bit so my response to his email was, "'Given my young age' ... compared to what? Is your doctor 95? lol Seriously, thanks for letting us know. Please let us know what you learn next, when you'll have the surgery, etc."

Did you catch my dad's casual mention of the anniversary of his near death? He tossed it into his email the way most people mention a high-school reunion. People who have served in the military normally don't like to talk about their combat experiences in casual daily conversations. Dad was no exception, but occasionally he'd let us in by relating a story. Here's the unabridged version in Dad's own words about what happened on January 5, 1966:

"After several months as a company commander, I was reassigned to the battalion staff as S-2, Intelligence Officer. Shortly thereafter, we mounted a regimental size operation against a large force of VC and North Vietnamese regulars planning an attack on Danang. The operation was named Long Lance and targeted the VC forces along the Song Vu Gai River valley south of Danang. To move the regiment as quickly as possible, the 1st Air Cavalry loaned us their helicopters. I was in the second wave of choppers with the battalion command group. That was a random choice in order to confuse the enemy as to the flight containing the command group. The first flight had landed without incident. It appeared that the NVA (North Vietnamese Army) regiment reported to be in the area had moved out.

As the second wave touched down, small arms fire raked the landing zone (LZ), followed by enemy mortar fire. I had not taken two steps from my chopper, and I was airborne on a mortar blast that landed several feet away. I never heard a thing. No blast. No sound of incoming fire. Just the sensation of flying through the air and an ache in my back. [Addition from Tom Vanderzyl who served with my father: I saw (your father) our Skipper being blown up and flying through the air with four other guys. He picked himself up, dusted himself off, saluted and headed up the hill as did Corporal Paskoski, who got a Purple Heart.]

Due to the heavy fire, downed choppers and wounded in the LZ (Landing Zone), the incoming

Marines had to jump from the choppers in order to land.

Mangled bodies were strewn across the LZ. I thought to myself, *"How can a leg be here without all the other parts?"* Blood soaked the rice paddy and the cry, *"Corpsman"* came from every direction.

In less than a minute, the quiet rice paddy had been turned into a killing zone. The mortar and small arms fire became more intense, and the bullwhip crack of passing bullets laced the air. The dull whomp, whomp, of mortar fire continued as the NVA attempted to close down the LZ and strand those Marines who had already landed. More people died and confusion reigned.

The attack wounded our battalion commander and three other battalion officers who had to be evacuated out of the area. That left me, the S-4 and another officer and the battalion sergeant major to run the battalion until replacements arrived about four hours later. To be truthful, those were the most terrifying moments of my life."

As I ponder that vivid battlefield scene, I can only imagine how that event, and other similar scenes, forged my dad into the person he became. No wonder he remembered the anniversary of that day 54 years later.

His grit and toughness were major reasons his passing seemed surreal to me. It didn't seem possible that he could be gone because he was the toughest person I knew. I understood in my head that someday he would die because none of us escapes that fate. But in my heart, I never really imagined it would happen. If you're blessed to not lose a parent when you're young, you'll discover the longer they live the more you assume they'll always be there. Until that day, both of my parents were alive, and I became conscious of the fact that I didn't know life apart from them. Every day of my life they'd been available to me. Even though I didn't see Dad much (usually once a year because of distance) and we didn't talk a lot on the phone, I always knew he was there if I needed him.

Like Dad, I'm a very early riser and have been most of my adult life. It's my time to run, work out, read, or walk and pray. When I do those activities, I'm by myself. Jane is never up when I take my walks. Knowing she is upstairs sleeping gives me a sense of peace and comfort. If she happens to be in Pennsylvania to spend time with her family, I feel alone on those mornings. That's how I suddenly felt about my father. Even though we didn't see each other often or talk much, there was a certain comfort knowing he was there, and I could reach out to him whenever I wanted to.

I said he was the toughest person I knew. He'd survived 13 months in the jungles of Vietnam during the war. He'd been in combat and was wounded by shrapnel. Although he never specifically mentioned killing people during the war, I'm pretty sure he did. You'll read more about his experiences in his own words later in the book.

A vivid memory I have of Dad was when I was seven or eight years old. It was the early 1970s and we lived in Southern California. My parents had my sister and me when they were very young, so Dad was only around 30 years old at the time of this memory. We spent a lot of weekends at the beach. We regularly visited Newport, Laguna, Malibu, and Huntington.

One summer day, we were at the beach and Dad was playing a pickup game of football with some college guys. Dad was only a few years removed from his service in the Marines, so he was still in great shape and very athletic. To say he was intense about whatever he did is an understatement. I remember hearing one of the guys say something like, *"Man, you should try out for the Rams!"* The Rams have bopped around the country over the decades but at the time they were the Los Angeles Rams. Thus, the reference by the college guy. When I was a kid, the Rams were my favorite team. Their quarterback, Roman Gabriel, was my favorite player. Like many youngsters, I wanted to grow up to be a professional football player so imagine how proud I was to hear that about Dad!

I'd heard stories from Dad's brothers and other people about him shooting pool and getting into bar fights. How could this strong, tough person suddenly be gone? As I sorted through some of his old files and photos, I discovered the following that he wrote about his life shortly after turning 79, less than six months from his death:

"And now I am beginning my 80th orbit of the sun. I am happy, I have wonderful memories but along came the COVID19. A virus affecting the world. Again, the world changed. Our economy and those around the world were in free fall in slightly more than 30 days. Hundreds of thousands died of the virus. 80 years is a long time but as one man said, *'It was in the blink of the eye.* "'

Ahearn Family Dynamics

> *"Honor your father and your mother."*
> —Exodus 20:12 (NASB®)

To understand someone better, get to know their family dynamics. Our family of origin is one of the most impactful factors that shapes who we are as human beings. John Bargh highlights this reality in his book, *Before You Know It*. The behavioral patterns that repeated themselves in the Ahearn family through the years helped me relate this story in writing. More importantly, the patterns and habits of our family helped me understand and empathize with my dad much more.

Dad was born on April 22, 1941, in the Bronx, NY, the second of what would eventually be seven children, to Cornelius and Helene Ahearn. My grandfather Cornelius was a first-generation Irish Catholic. My grandmother Helene's maiden name was Seiz. She was of German descent. Their first child was Cornelius, known to everyone as Corny. Then it was my father Brian, followed by Kevin, Barry, Denis, and Rory. Last, but by no means least, they had a little girl they named Eileen.

As a kid I loved being around my uncles! They were quintessential Irish Catholics. In their case, the Hollywood stereotype was true. They drank too much, swore a lot, fought like cats and dogs, and told raunchy jokes. They all had major issues with their father. They loved and adored their mother but had no problem setting her hair on fire with worry. They added anxiety to her life any way they could. If sainthood can be earned, then my grandmother is a saint thanks to her boys.

I remember being at family gatherings, listening intently to Dad and his brothers telling jokes so I could retell them to all of my friends at school. In second grade my mother had to come to school to meet with the principal because of a joke I'd overheard then retold. The joke was immature and crude. I still remember the punchline, but I'll spare you the details. I had no idea what the joke meant. All I knew was Dad and his brothers thought it was hilarious, and that was good enough for me. The point is, I looked up to my dad and uncles. I wanted to be like them, even if I got into trouble sometimes following their example.

When I was in second grade, I had to write an essay about my parents. I wrote about one of our frequent beach trips. They took my sister Carey and me to Lee's Bar, where we played pool and slot machines (nickel and penny). If the essay were written today, child protection services would be knocking on my parents' door. For California in the early 1970s, it was no big deal.

My grandmother was a devout Catholic woman. She hoped and prayed at least one of her boys would become a priest. That didn't happen despite their Catholic upbringing and attending Catholic schools. In spite of all the hell they raised, I do believe those early years instilled a deep sense of right and wrong in each of them, and their mother (my grandmother) had a profound impact on them. My father wrote this about his mother:

> "What was most positive in our lives was Mom. She was absolutely the best person who ever lived. Think of it. She coped with him (Dad) and kept us on the straight and narrow and out of his way. When he wasn't there, she was the rock. It would have been easy for her to complain but it wasn't in her to do that. She was always loving and accepted as part of the family anyone we brought into it. She was what was happy and great about our family. Her goodness outshined all the bad times with Dad."

My grandfather was wicked smart. He was a college professor at Columbia, Fordham, NYU, and Baruch College. He also worked for various businesses during his career. Accounting was his thing. There was a high premium on education in the Ahearn family and that was apparent by the professions many chose. Corny was an attorney. Dad taught at a few colleges in Florida after he retired from business. Barry and Denis both taught high school. Kevin had a short stint teaching at the high school level and eventually started his own real estate training business. My sister Carey is an elementary school librarian in Arizona. I was involved in corporate training for more than 20 years, headed up a corporate university, and now run my own training and consulting business. Some of my cousins are in learning related fields too. Education is a high priority in the Ahearn family, and it started with my grandfather. When I was promoted to Learning Director for State Auto University Dad sent me the following congratulatory email:

> "And so the tradition goes on:
> My dad was a Dean at City College in NY,
> I was a Dean at Keiser University,
> And now you.
> Well deserved."

Unfortunately, my grandfather also set the tone for something else—*"a fondness for the grape"*—as my uncle Rory put it. Over the course of time, each of my father's siblings, with the exception of himself and Kevin, would have to come to grips with alcoholism. Thankfully, they all found help in AA. At a family reunion in 2012, I recall each of them being just as much fun as I remembered when I was a kid, even though alcohol was no longer involved. They were just a fun, rowdy bunch with unbelievable stories.

My grandfather's drinking and aloofness led each brother as well as their sister Eileen to experience a host of issues. I can speak to the impact I observed with Dad, supplemented from what little he shared, stories his brothers recounted, and what I gathered from Mom, Ann, who was married to him for 20 years. Regarding his father's drinking, Dad wrote:

"He treated Mom poorly. At one point he was so drunkenly abusive I told him I would kill him if he laid a hand on Mom. I recall telling her that she should divorce him or throw him out of the house."

"As badly as he [sic: my grandfather Cornelius] treated Mom and the kids, he had a stellar reputation with some of my friends. They remember his help 50 years later. Dan Lynch was bailed out of New Rochelle jail for stealing (borrowing) a rowboat from docks near The Barge. Others have said he gave them special help. I cannot say that it was extended to me."

The irony in learning about that incident between Dad and his father was I realized history had repeated itself. My father was verbally and physically abusive to my mother at different times during their rocky relationship. She ended up throwing him out of the house as a result of the abuse and his infidelity. You'll see many instances of history repeating itself throughout this book. We don't just inherit genes from our parents, there's a social inheritance as well, for both good and bad.

I think being the second son was hard on my father. Corny was the first born and his father's namesake, so Dad grew up directly in Corny's shadow. Corny played piano, loved opera, and spoke Italian and French. Dad was into fishing, trapping, and hunting. There were racoon pelts hung in the garage, the trophies of his expertise in the woods. In many respects it was hard to believe they were brothers because they were so different.

My grandmother Helene recounted, if Corny got a 95 on a test my grandfather would respond, *"Why not a 100? You're an Ahearn!"* My Uncle Rory said, *"Corny's battles with my grandfather were the things of legend, two stubborn Irishmen who only saw their worst reflection in each other."*

According to my grandmother, my father understood at an early age that confrontation with the *"Old Man"* was fruitless, so he just went about doing whatever he wanted on the down low. All the while, my grandfather fixated on Corny's seemingly endless misdeeds, and as a result, my grandfather paid little attention to Dad. Regarding this time period my father wrote:

> "His drinking became more apparent to me in the 50s while I was at Iona [sic: Preparatory High School]. He and Corny fought frequently, usually when Dad was drinking. Dad put unreasonable demands on Corny such as, be home from a dance at 9:30 pm. Corny, instead of agreeing, knowing that Dad would be out [sic: drunk] by 8 pm, argued. I learned. I agreed then stayed out until 1 am."

In high school, academic achievement wasn't a priority for Dad, even though it was a big deal for his father. I recall Dad telling me he graduated 121st of 123 in his class at Iona Prep School in New Rochelle, NY. Despite his poor academic showing, he was smart and that became apparent in college. He buckled down and he graduated with honors from Fairfield College (now University). It was then that Dad realized he was very intelligent and that became a big part of his identity, something people always noted about him. The following incident comes directly from something my father wrote later in life about that period:

"I admit, I was not the brightest bulb in the lamp, and I deserved what I got most of the time.

My saddest recollection was when I was struggling to get into Fairfield and failed Trig for the third time! Mom begged the dean of admissions to accept me on a trial basis. In August of 1958, prior to leaving for college, Dad invited me to lunch in the city. We went to lunch at the Villa d'Este. I waited outside his office talking with Grace Fierro, his long-time secretary. As we waited, Dad was finishing a conversation with one of his fellow workers.

The man asked, 'How is Brian doing?'

Dad answered, 'He got accepted conditionally to Fairfield, but he won't last six months. Then he's off to The Marines.'

Poor Grace. She teared up and squeezed my hand. We had lunch and he corrected me on how to properly eat a roll in a restaurant like Villa d'Este. I never again ate a roll in one bite.

While it was a sh*t moment at the time, I think I decided that I would show him, which I did. I think he was shocked when I decided to enter The Marine Corps after graduation. We had a brief talk that centered on me being a Supply Officer. I ended up in the infantry.

I had no contact with him from 1962 until I returned from Nam [sic: 1966]. He hadn't changed much."

Despite the tension between Dad and his father, I believe my grandfather loved him and was proud of him, even if he couldn't acknowledge his feelings about my dad. At my father's funeral his youngest brother Rory said their father *"gave up the grape"* the day Dad left for Vietnam and remained sober until he returned home safely. I think his deep Catholic roots caused him to look upward for protection for his son. The father-son tension, and the drinking, resumed once Dad was home safely and the tension continued until my grandfather passed away in 1978, at just 66 years old. I never understood what was at the core of their relationship and my father was not one to talk about it. Dad wrote the following about his father:

"In the early 1970s I was made VP General Manager of a company in Connecticut. He [sic: my grandfather] was somewhat impressed but in my opinion never gave much praise."

Whenever I asked Dad about growing up it was always fun stories about parties and friends, the kinds of things I observed as a kid at family gatherings. Dad never mentioned how his father tossed all of his clothes out of a second-floor window onto the front lawn in a drunken fit of anger. I heard about that from my mother. That, and I'm sure many other similar incidents arising from his father's drinking, *had* to affect my father. How could it not? I think Dad just shoved those thoughts away because, when I brought the clothing incident up, it was apparent to me that he'd never thought deeply about how it impacted him and his other relationships. Later in life Dad summed up his father with these words:

"If I were to sum it up, I would say that Dad was an overachiever driven by the fact that he and brother Daniel were the children of immigrants. Think of it this way, they were the Latinos of the early 20th century! The Irish lived in enclaves and were looked down upon. Their parents were barely educated immigrants, earning a living in the most menial of jobs, maid, and carpenter-mason. I would imagine there was some resentment. I would imagine that they wanted to get out of the rut as soon as possible. They did it through education, much to the credit of their parents. Perhaps that was the origin of *'Be the best.'* Read *'The Race.'* Both he and Danny were alcoholics and did very little about it. I believe booze to them was a crutch behind which they could hide deeper fears."

My Family

"The Lord is slow to anger and abundant in mercy, forgiving wrongdoing and violation of His Law; but He will by no means leave the guilty unpunished, inflicting the punishment of the fathers on the children to the third and the fourth generations."
—Numbers 14:18 (NASB®)

The Beginning

My father and mother, Ann, were married on June 18, 1962, in New Rochelle, NY. My sister Carey entered the picture on January 16, 1963, while Dad was going through his Marine Corps training in Quantico, Virginia. If you do the math on that you'll realize Mom was pregnant before they tied the knot. It wasn't a family secret, but I never realized that until I was an adult. They'd not dated too long at that point, so the pregnancy was a big factor in the decision to get married. It's what most people did back then under those circumstances.

During one of our difficult conversations later in life, Dad made a comment that stuck with me and revealed a lot about his views on church. Despite his Catholic upbringing, which included being an altar boy and Catholic schools, after the war he wanted nothing to do with the church. He said something to the effect, "You're raised your whole life going to church then when you need help the priest says, 'Go away. We don't want to deal with that.'" I surmised what he was talking about. He turned to the church for guidance when he found out Mom was pregnant but there were no answers, no offers to help in any way. I can't blame him for the feelings he harbored regarding the church because if there's one place you'd expect to provide help and guidance in difficult times it would be the church.

I joined the family on April 1, 1964. I was given Dad's name but to avoid confusion with Dad I was affectionately called Breenie or Breen by everyone in the family. Breen is a common last name for many Irish families and Dad had a friend with that name. And yes, I'm an April Fool but I always tell people, "I may be a fool but I'm not stupid." I was born in Tripler Army Hospital in Honolulu, Hawaii. My father was stationed at the Marine Corps Base on Kaneohe Bay after basic training, prior to heading off to Vietnam. That's where Mom remained while he was overseas for more than a year. Living in Hawaii might seem glamorous, but it was tough on Mom because she was a 21-year-old with a toddler and infant, had no family around, and only other young Marine moms to lean on. As I noted earlier, you'll read about Dad's time in The Corps in his own words later in the book.

By late 1966 we were stateside, back in New Rochelle, NY, with my parents' families. I have vague memories of that time, and most are supplemented with old photos and stories. During that time my father started his business career with General Mills. In the summer of 1969, we drove across the country to California because Dad had been offered a transfer. Who wouldn't have wanted to live in Southern California in the late 60s and early 70s! It was nothing like it is now. Back then it was very laid back, sun and fun, and both of my parents were in their late 20s, barely more than kids raising kids.

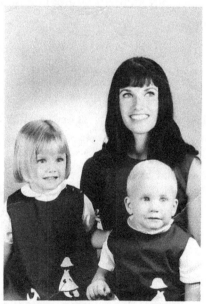

Carey and me with Mom in 1966

California Here We Come

During our four years in California, we lived in four spots in Orange County and my parents were separated half of the time. I was so young I didn't think anything of the moves nor Dad not always living with us. My sister, being nearly a year and a half older than me, has many more memories.

I came to learn much later in life that my Dad was running around on Mom before we left New York as well as during those California years. According to Mom, he even had his secretary transferred to California because he was having an affair with her.

At his funeral, Dad's brother Kevin told me a story that encapsulated Dad during that time. Kevin had flown out for an interview Dad arranged for him. Kevin said my father picked him up at the airport Friday afternoon, but they didn't make it to our house until Sunday! From the airport Kevin said they went straight to bars, pool halls, strip clubs, slept on the beach, and then repeated everything on Saturday. While it might have made a good scene for the movie *The Hangover*, I told Kevin, "*And that's why my Mom was angry with him so much of their marriage.*" In a moment of clarity, he agreed she had the right to be.

My sister, probably seven or eight years old at the time, vividly remembers seeing an altercation between my Mom, Dad, and another woman who was in his apartment when we arrived unannounced. This occurred during a "*surprise*" visit from the three of us while Mom and Dad were separated. I think Mom, understandably, wanted to check up on him. Who could blame her? According to Carey there was screaming, and a physical altercation ensued when Mom slapped the other woman. I don't know if I was just too young to remember it or if I blocked it out. No matter, it was a vivid memory for Carey.

Regarding my sister, Mom said when I came along Dad paid very little attention to her going forward. I don't know if it was a conscious choice on his part or not. Perhaps it was a sign of the times, a man taking more pride in his son. Whatever the reasons, I believe neglect from her father, and the abuse Carey observed, had a big impact on her view of men.

From my earliest memories, Dad had a temper and didn't like to be confronted or questioned. When his temper flared it was scary and took everyone back who was present. I suspect the mix of feisty Irish blood, the angry outbursts of an alcoholic father, Marine Corps training, and what he experienced in combat had a lot to do with his intensity. During one of those intense occasions, Carey remembers seeing him strike Mom in the car, bloodying her nose in the process. Unfortunately, according to Mom, there were numerous other instances like that, and some were even more violent. I was in the car too; but again, no memory at all. Despite not remembering, I'm sure incidents like that affected me too.

Having grown and learned much, I now understand my father was struggling with PTSD (post-traumatic stress disorder) during those years. I don't think he could have acknowledged it at the time for several reasons. First of all, PTSD was not something people were talking about back then and it can be difficult to acknowledge something which lacks a label. Another reason is, because it's hard to have perspective on one's own behavior when you're in the middle of it.

On top of that, while many vets were struggling just to hold a job, Dad was doing well in his career. Nonetheless, without a positive role model growing up, chasing women, drinking, staying out late to shoot pool, and getting in occasional bar fights, were probably his way of dealing with the bottled-up emotions from his Vietnam experience. Regarding PTSD, Dad wrote:

> "Much has been said over the years about Post Traumatic Stress Disorder (PTSD) and its impact on those who served in Vietnam and other wars. It is real and it is there every day. Some let it show all the time while others bury it deep inside. In either case, it is there and always will be. The glory that we ascribe to the John Waynes of the world does not entail the pain that endures because of brothers lost."

It was during those California years that Dad was befriended by a man named John Bowling in California. John was in his 50s and probably represented a father figure to Dad. He's the one Dad shot pool with and ran around with. I remember learning to ride a motorcycle around my eighth birthday with Dad, John, and John's son. What Dad may never have known was that John tried to seduce my mother once, doing his best to convince her to spend the night with him when we (Mom, Carey, and I) were at his place for dinner. So much for "friends."

Dad told me, much later in life, when we were discussing religion, that after all he saw and experienced in Vietnam he thought, "All that crap (religion) can't be real." When the moral compass is removed, one can justify almost anything. After all, if there's no true right or wrong then we might as well follow the Greek philosopher Epicurus's advice to *"eat, drink, and be merry because tomorrow we may die."*

Regarding that time in California, a few special memories with Dad stand out. In 1971 he took me to the L.A. Coliseum to watch the USC Trojans take on the UCLA Bruins in the "crosstown rivalry" football game. We had burgers before the game at Stubby's Trojan Barrel, a bar owned by a former Los Angeles Rams football player Marlin McKeever. Neither team was very good that year and it was a lackluster game, ending in a low scoring tie. However, as a seven-year-old that didn't matter because I was with Dad and got to experience the sights, sounds, and pageantry of big-time college football in a historic venue. More than 50 years later I still have the program he bought that day for me.

Just a few weeks later Dad took me to my first professional football game. We were back in The Coliseum to watch the Los Angeles Rams, my favorite team at the time, play the New Orleans Saints. I remember that game well because Willie Ellison, the Rams' running back, broke Jim Brown's single game NFL rushing record. Another memorable experience and game.

The following year Dad and I returned to The Coliseum to watch USC trounce Notre Dame 45–23. USC went on to beat Ohio State in the Rose Bowl, finishing the season undefeated and the Trojans were named consensus national champions.

Despite all that was happening with my parents, and Dad not being around much, as I reflect on everything, I believe he was doing his best to be a good father to me.

Before leaving California in 1973, my parents had reconciled and purchased their first home in Costa Mesa. After two years in different apartments with Mom and Carey, it was great to have a real house and Dad around all of the time. This was our fourth place in Southern California in just four years. We weren't in that home a full year and it was time to move again because of Dad's work. By this time, I was used to moving, having been at four different schools during our time in California, so I wasn't fazed by the news. In fact, I was excited because we were moving back East which meant we would see my grandparents, aunts, and uncles more often.

Back East

We ended up back East, settling in Simsbury, Connecticut, just outside of Hartford. I recall those years with fond memories. I had a good group of friends, some of whom I stay in touch with decades later thanks to social media. Little

League football, basketball, and baseball dominated our days. When my friends and I weren't outside, we were playing Risk, Stratego, Monopoly, and other board games to fill our time. Although I was getting older, I still had no clue about the struggles my parents were having in their marriage. My sister was far more observant and inquisitive than I was. Later in life when I looked back, I could see hints, but from ages nine through 12, I was absorbed in the things boys typically did back then—in being a child.

A pivotal moment with Dad came when I was 11 years old. I'd agreed to cut our next-door neighbor's grass. The lawnmower we had was an old piece of junk and rocks and debris kept flying out from underneath, hitting my exposed legs on a hot summer day. In frustration I quit. For that move I was grounded and spent the weekend in my bedroom. The message from Dad was clear: Once you start something you never quit. I suspect that came from being a Marine: always complete your mission. No kid likes being disciplined but I never forgot it and with the passage of time I've come to realize that lesson has paid huge dividends in my life.

Despite all that was still going on with my parents, I do have some good memories with Dad from those Connecticut days. One of the best was a two-week period where I went jogging with Dad in the morning. He'd tell me stories about being in the Marines and basic training. I distinctly remember him talking about Billy Mills, the Native American distance runner who won Olympic gold in the 10,000-meter race during the 1964 Olympics in Tokyo. Mills was a long shot who came from nowhere, beating his personal best by nearly 50 seconds, to upset Australia's Ron Clarke, the world record holder. Mills was in boot camp at the same time as Dad and Dad said he'd always finish runs 10 to 20 minutes ahead of everyone else. I don't recall why those morning runs ended but it's likely that we got out of the routine when Dad's travels across the country and around the world resumed.

I recall Dad traveling to various places in Asia, South America, and Europe for work. Sometimes he would send postcards from the cities he visited. I continued that tradition with Abigail. When she was little, I'd send postcards from wherever I traveled to, and I'd usually pick up a small present for her. I know that meant a lot to her because, on her wedding day when I walked into the parlor to see her for the first time, she had all of the postcards displayed on a table. That brought me to tears.

Another fond memory was Dad's involvement when I played little league football. As a kid, he was at most of my midweek practices and Saturday morning games. When I played high school football he was always at games if he wasn't traveling for work. Despite his intensity, he wasn't a "little league" parent. I never recall him making a scene nor questioning coaches—like too many parents do today.

I enjoyed that father-son time because, looking back on it, I didn't get much of that one-on-one time compared to my friends who seemed to have more stable homes. I think that's part of the reason I was so intent on spending father-daughter time with Abigail, our first and only child, when she came along.

On to Dublin, Ohio

After three quick years in Simsbury, it was time for yet another move. It was March 1977, I was in seventh grade, and Dad's work took us to Dublin, Ohio. Dublin was tiny! There were a few gas stations and antique shops in the "downtown" area and not much else. But the town was about to explode because Jack Nicklaus built Muirfield Village Golf Course there. In 1976 his Memorial Golf Tournament had its inaugural PGA event. To put the growth that ensued in perspective, according to the 1970 census there were less than 700 residents in Dublin, and 50 years later the population was just a hair under 50,000.

Shortly after the move my grandmother and grandfather flew out from New York to visit us. Whatever issues were there between Dad and his father, it was clear they had not been resolved. Their interaction was so toxic that the visit was cut short and my grandparents went home early.

I don't know precisely why the relationship between my father and grandfather was so bad and my father never talked about it. As a teenager I didn't broach the subject, and I never did later in life. Whenever I asked him about growing up all he talked about were parties at the house and the fun shenanigans he and his brothers got into. Certainly, my grandfather's alcoholism, which continued until his death about six months after that visit, the treatment of my grandmother, and my grandfather's harsh stance with all of the Ahearn kids were factors.

Regarding the death of his father, Dad seemed dispassionate about it when he wrote the following:

> "I moved to Ohio in 1977 and he died the following year. I was notified by my secretary while I was conducting a meeting of our division presidents. I told her to get me tickets to NYC and I finished the meeting."

Having served in Vietnam, I think it bothered Dad that my grandfather didn't serve in some capacity during WWII. I came across the following email Dad sent to his brother-in-law Gary, a Marine who married Dad's only sister, Eileen. Dad was trying to track down a letter he believed Eileen had in her possession. It was something my grandmother had written to the kids regarding their father not serving.

"As we all know, Eileen was a packrat of Ahearn family information, pictures, letters, etc. Years ago, she, or one of my brothers, shared a letter my mom had written to the boys. It appeared to be written in the late 1940s. Eileen was yet to be born. WWII was not long over, and she [sic: Dad's mother] was trying to explain why my father had not entered the service during the war. At that time, many of us had schoolmates who had lost fathers in the war, and it was possible that our questions drove her to write the letter.

She never shared the letter with us, and it was found among her papers after her death. The tone of it was apologetic, focusing on dad's love for his family as his reason for not serving in the war. You could tell by her words that she was defending him. It was a sad letter and over the years it has intrigued me to see and read it again."

On the subject of drinking in the Ahearn family, I never observed Dad drunk and, unlike most of his siblings, alcohol didn't take over his life. I'm fortunate that it's never been an issue for me either. In high school and college I drank, and I still enjoy Scotch, but have never felt it was an issue.

I was blessed to find another great group of friends in Dublin. The town was growing, but with fewer than 200 kids in my high school class we all knew each other, and I remain close to many people from those years.

Something that had a profound impact on me took place when I was in eighth grade. I brought home a grade card with six As and one C. Dad looked at it and said, "*What happened in English?*" It wasn't in a mean tone, but it did set something in motion in me—nothing short of perfect was good enough. Perfectionism dogged me for the better part of my life, and I tie it back to that seemingly innocent comment. Unknowingly, Dad had done to me, albeit in a much milder way, what his father did to Corny and the other Ahearn boys.

When our daughter Abigail was a freshman in high school, Jane and I went to an open house during her first semester. Abigail never liked school, but she was doing well, mostly As and Bs, but she had a D going in science at the time. By then I'd learned a lot, so I bit my tongue because I didn't want her to feel the way I'd felt all those years ago. We talked about the importance of school and Abigail always did what was necessary to keep moving ahead. I was especially proud of her when, during college she failed a math class twice but signed up for a third time and passed the class. As a sign language major, math had little to do with interacting with the deaf community, but she knew it was necessary to graduate so she persisted. To put a positive spin on it I told her, when you interview for a job and someone asks about a weakness you can say, "*Math! I failed a class twice, but I wasn't about to let that stop me from working with the deaf community!*"

Dad became obsessed with golf because we lived in the Muirfield neighborhood, in the shadow of Jack Nicklaus's golf course, and Dad's company had a corporate membership to the golf club. He had a five-minute walk to the driving range, so hitting balls or playing was a daily thing when he wasn't traveling. I think golf was another outlet for him because the game takes so much time and mental focus. I learned to play golf at Muirfield. Early on I enjoyed the game so much that I almost didn't play football my freshman year of high school because I contemplated trying out for the golf team. I decided to stick with football and I'm glad I did because of the lasting friendships I made and the discipline I learned. As head coach Todd Alles used to tell us, I learned a lot about life playing the game.

I mentioned earlier that my Dad was intense. That applied to everything he did, including golf. He eventually worked his way down to a single digit handicap. When I was an adult and we played on occasion, I cannot recall a time he shot 80 or higher. It was almost always 74 to 77 on his scorecard. When he got to the point where he couldn't play as well as he wanted, he left the game altogether to pursue his love of fishing. I think that's when he began to slow down, relax, and think more deeply.

I inherited intensity from my father. Whatever I chose to do in life I wanted to do it extremely well. That was apparent with weightlifting, running, and martial arts. My body took to weights like a duck to water! During and after college, I competed in powerlifting and bodybuilding contests. I made the radical shift to running marathons. I progressed so well that I qualified for and ran The Boston Marathon—twice. To spend time with our daughter Abigail, I joined Taekwondo and earned my 2nd degree black belt in less than five years.

Another example of my intensity came with church later in life. When I started to read the Bible, I wanted to under-stand it, so I began to write down my thoughts. Those thoughts became a sort of commentary that was well over 1,000 pages by the time I finished. My perfectionism, an unrealistic belief that I had to be right all the time, reared its head around then. Despite all of my Bible study, there was something I couldn't square away as I studied—the timing of the Passover dinner in the Gospel of John versus the other Gospel accounts. One night I was at a party and religion came up. The person I was talking with said, *"The Apostle John wasn't even a good Jew because he didn't get the timing of the Passover dinner correct."* Despite all of my study I had no answer. That night, while lying in bed, I told Jane I felt ashamed that I couldn't answer his objection, and I cried.

I'm thankful I've grown quite a bit since that time. I no longer feel the need to have all the answers. Now, when asked some questions, I'm comfortable telling people, "I don't know," or "I don't really have an opinion on that because I've not looked into it." I'm also okay saying, "You know what, I was wrong about that."

My sophomore year of high school we had to keep a journal for an English class. We all thought it was dumb initially, but I really got into writing. Between playing football, going to parties, dating, and all that my parents were going through, I filled up notebooks, writing hundreds of pages of handwritten accounts of teenage life. As I looked back on some of what I wrote I realized I was an angry kid. I wrote *"the f word"* a lot, would get set off by stupid things, and wrote passages about kids and teachers that I'm embarrassed about now. Sometimes I wonder, if a child psychologist read it today, would I have been classified as a troubled youth? Looking back, that journal was an outlet for me, the tool to let some air out of the balloon that seemingly was about to burst at times.

Concerning my family, I wrote we were just four people who shared the same roof. I felt like none of us had anything in common. Dad had work and golf, Mom was taking classes at Columbus College of Art & Design, Carey was into country music and studied like crazy, and I was into football, working out, and my girlfriend. I thought none of the family dynamics affected me. I was wrong.

It was November 9, 1979, my sophomore year in high school, and I'd been out with friends doing who knows what. I woke up in the middle of the night because I heard Mom and Dad yelling and screaming. Here's what I wrote in the journal I was keeping in English that year:

> "After I got home and went to bed, I heard my mom and dad fighting. It seems like once a year they really go at it. I tell you; it scared the piss out of me though. I don't see how they can have such a big fight. I never fight like that with Janis [sic: the girl I was dating] but then marriage is totally dif-

ferent. All I heard was my mom crying and yelling at dad. He kept telling her to shut up, only it was so loud it sounded like it was in stereo. When I went downstairs in the morning there were a bunch of broken coffee cups and dad was sleeping on the couch. A real knockdown, drag out. The thing that scares me is my dad might just get so mad one day he'll take my mom's head off without knowing it. There's a slight size difference between the two."

It turns out he was having another affair, and Mom wasn't going to put up with it any longer. I'm not sure exactly when she learned about it, but it came to her attention from a friend of hers who worked with Dad. He moved out the following Saturday, November 17, and I wrote in my journal:

"Well, dad moved out of the house. I didn't see him, but I heard him talking to my mom. I haven't seen him for nine days. Mom says if he asks me to go over for Thanksgiving I should feel free to go. I shouldn't spend it with either. I don't really know what to think or do. On the outside I try not to show anything, but I don't know what to think on the inside. My mom was asking me what I think about them getting a divorce. I told her to do what she wanted to do and I won't let it affect me, or I'll try not to let it. I also said he's still my dad and the only difference would be that he's not with us. But

I've been thinking about how it might affect me. I think my grades might go down without him pushing me or I could act like nothing happened and do normal. There are two sides to everything. I know that I'd start staying out late and stuff like that because he wouldn't be there expecting me home. My discipline will go down the drain, I know that. I guess I sometimes do things because I'm afraid of my dad but not my mom. Neither of them alone would have much control over me, they're too busy. But together, when one isn't looking after me the other is, so I don't get away with anything. Or, I would have to self-discipline myself, so I don't get f**ked over because of them. I guess I do need them pushing me. I realize you need all that stuff to be successful and I think I want to be successful. In that respect I admire my dad. He's come a long way but he's not successful in everything. This whole ordeal is proof. That's what I want to be most successful at, love or marriage. That's what I'm waiting for, the day I'm so in love that I get married."

I recall my sister and I went to a restaurant with him on Thanksgiving. It was the same awkward feeling I remembered from the times in California when he'd pick us up to spend time with us on weekends while my parents were separated. I don't think he was comfortable around us. It may have been the awkward situation we were in; it might have been the troubled past with his Dad, or it could have been something else. About that day I wrote, *"This is the absolute worst Thanksgiving I've ever had. I'm not looking forward to Christmas."*

Dad and Carey going to a father-daughter dance in January 1977.

During that time, he was going to Florida around Christmas. Mom said we should go if he offered to take us. I was hoping he wouldn't ask me or my sister to go because I was dating someone and, like any 15-year-old, I wanted to spend time with my girlfriend over the holidays. However, when he didn't ask it was disappointing because it sent a signal that he'd rather not spend time with us. I still don't get Dad's perspective. In contrast, when our daughter Abigail was born, all I wanted to do was spend time with her. For example, I would get her out of the crib in the early morning to read to her. When I was doing chores around the house, I would cradle her in one arm just to be with her. Until she was 17 years old and told me to stop because I was waking her up, each morning I would crack open her door when I was up around four a.m. and I'd whisper, "*I love you.*" To this day, some of my favorite times are those where Abigail asks me to go to a coffee shop or the mall just to hang out together and talk.

Later during my sophomore year another incident took place that, in hindsight, was actually quite funny, but not so much at the time. Shortly after my 16th birthday I wrecked the driver's ed car! As if that wasn't bad enough, it took place right in front of the high school during lunch which meant everyone found out about it immediately. That's a hard one to live down and I felt like a fool. When classmates teased me, I went along but inside it really bothered me. I had to go to court with Dad because of the accident and the fact that I only had a learner's permit. My first court appearance was a good learning experience and turned out to be, in retrospect, my first step into a career around influence. On April 30, 1980, I wrote in my journal:

"I went to court and the judge was pretty cool. I pleaded no contest and told him everything. He said I was still guilty but under the circumstances he'd throw the ticket out, so I didn't have to pay a fine and still have no points [sic: on my driving record]. I think my dad was happier about it than I was. He just wanted to pay the fine and leave but I was curious and wanted to see the judge. I guess my curiosity paid off."

My junior year I started on the football team and was selected as a captain before our senior season. That's when I got into working out more intensely. A group of us football players drove to the downtown Columbus YMCA three days a week to participate in a high school weightlifting program with some kids who played football for an inner-city high school. It was a culture shock for us suburban kids, and I think it was for the kids from South High School too. Working out the year before, I'd only gained a measly five pounds. However, when we learned how to work out from competitive powerlifters, I put on more than 20 pounds in three months. I was hooked! I was 17 years old, getting noticeably bigger and stronger, and people began to comment on the change. It became a big part of my identity. I owe a lot to Steve Grill and Walt Sword, a couple of powerlifters who ran the program at the YMCA, for taking an active interest in me at that time and throughout college. During college breaks and summers, I worked out with them and occasionally joined them and other lifters socially. In hindsight, I was looking for older, male approval so they, along with my football coaches, filled a huge void for me. I credit weightlifting for keeping me on the straight and narrow during that time.

Towards the end of my junior year there was an incident that profoundly impacted me. I was in the library and was talking when I wasn't supposed to, so the librarian confronted me. She was a nice lady who had a great relationship with my sister, and she liked me too. When she called me out, I defended myself like most teenage guys would. She commented that I'd talked the previous day as well. I reminded her it was a teacher I talked with the day before. She didn't like that, so she said, "If you don't like it then leave." I stood up and exploded, saying loud enough for everyone to hear, "Fine! I don't give a d**n! I'm gonna get the hell out of here!" I marched out one door and she marched out the other and summoned me to an empty class-room. To her credit, she gave me every opportunity to apol-ogize, but I wouldn't give her the satisfaction. That incident got me a three-day suspension, killed any chance at National Honor Society, and almost cost me being a captain on the foot-ball team. That would have crushed me. I give a lot of credit to Head Coach Todd Alles for talking with me and giving me a second chance. He was more about molding the character of his players than the wins and losses. Dublin was a small town and I think he knew what was going on with me and at home. I'm thankful to say, more than 40 years after graduating, I still maintain a close relationship with Coach Alles.

If you would have told me at the time, "I think your out-burst has to do with your parents," my response would have been, "It has nothing to do with that. She (the librarian) is just a b**ch!" That's how I felt and what I believed at that time. I look back now and realize my anger had EVERYTHING to do with what was happening at home. So often we have no clue why we do what we do, even as adults. In the moment we try to assign meaning, but at 17 years old I was clueless about the depth of the struggles my parents were dealing with and how it was impacting me. I'm thankful I came to that realization before Abigail came along. I've shared that story with her, and it's been a teaching point that's helped her have more compassion for people who engage in certain self-destructive behaviors. I think Abigail had more understanding and empathy for kids in high school knowing what I went through.

While on the subject of the suspension, thanks to the internet, just recently I was able to locate Linda Roosa, the librarian. I called her and apologized for my behavior. She was so gracious and acknowledged, had I apologized at the time, nothing more would have happened. Fortunately, I learned to apologize long ago. As Dale Carnegie, author of *How to Win Friends and Influence People*, wrote, "When you're wrong, admit it *quickly and emphatically.*" That's good advice and, in my case, better late than never!

Another angry outburst happened around that time with my sister. When it came to personalities, she was very much like Dad and didn't take crap from anyone. In turn, I didn't take her crap and we fought continually as kids. When I say we fought, at times it was physical. During one of those fights, I was in seventh grade and she was in eighth, I broke my right hand when I punched her. My punishment was self-imposed as I miss the last half of the football season.

One day, during my senior year of high school, we got in an argument, no idea over what, and I went berserk. I yanked her straight to the floor by the collar of her shirt. She retaliated so I chased her up the stairs into Mom's bedroom. I was about to hit her when Mom came in. I remember the look on her face. It was fear because she knew I was no longer her little boy that she could control. I was only 5-foot-9 but had gone from 155 to 190 pounds of muscle in about a year and a half from all the weightlifting. Dad came over the next day to talk to me. Surprisingly, it was a good talk and didn't result in any punishment that I can remember.

My sister and I now have a wonderful relationship because she's an incredibly kind and loving person. We're very different in many respects but we share a love of Scotch and cigars. On top of that, she's so much fun to be around because she has such varied interests.

Stepping Out of His Shadow

> *"There are three things extremely hard;*
> *steel, a diamond, and to know one's self."*
> —Ben Franklin

Miami University

A couple of battles that stand out with Dad had to do with college. Because of the value the family placed on education it was expected that Carey and I would go to college. Dad said he'd pay for any in-state college because out-of-state tuition was too expensive. Despite the fact that there were lots of very good schools in Ohio, Carey had her heart set on American University in Washington, D.C. When Dad said he couldn't afford it, she said it was because he'd spent his money on Jo. They were not married at the time, so Jo was *the other woman.*" There were lots of expletives exchanged between Dad and Carey as two very similar, very stubborn people felt they were in the right. It was the type of interaction my grandfather had with Corny and probably my father.

The summer of 1982 I got ready to head off to college at Miami University, located in Southwest, Ohio, a two-hour drive from Dublin—far enough to be away but close enough to get home whenever I wanted. Dad had been living with Jo for several years and they would get married later that fall. He and Jo took me down for my freshman orientation. I was so into weightlifting that my thought for college was to learn all I could so I could open my own gym someday. I don't recall this, but Jo said Dad and I had a really intense conversation—one that included a lot of yelling—about my major as we stood by the car. I remember having the conversation but not that it was intense. Perhaps the intensity was just normal for us and didn't stand out in any significant way.

He was paying for school and wanted me to study business. I must have been leaning towards physical education or something else I thought would be more in line with opening a gym. I relented and became a general business major. I decided that would be the most well-rounded approach rather than pigeonholing myself into accounting, finance, or some other discipline. You'll recall, my grandfather insisted Dad study accounting in college. I don't know what he would have studied if he could have freely chosen. History was repeating itself once again.

Shortly after arriving at college in August 1982, my parents' divorce was finalized. I don't remember when Dad filed for the divorce, but I do recall that Mom found out when a friend saw the filing in the local paper and called her. Despite the fact that Dad had been out of the house for quite some time when he filed, and was living with Jo, I think deep down Mom thought it might still work out somehow. It was a slap in the face, complete lack of respect that he didn't tell her he was taking that final step. Mom said he asked for an annulment because he wanted to get married in the Catholic Church. Her response, *"So you're saying our kids are bastards?"* She didn't relent but nonetheless, on September 11, 1982, Dad married Jo in a small ceremony in Dublin.

Regarding the wedding, my freshman year of college I kept a journal and came across this entry from September 2, 1982, *"Sharon [sic: a friend whose parents knew my dad] called me and said her mom told her Jo and my dad are getting married on September 11. I love finding out second hand.*" Apparently Mom wasn't the only one who found out from friends what was going on with him. Dad called four days later to tell me about the wedding and asked that I come home for the ceremony.

I didn't have a car at college and being over two hours away I wasn't going to make the wedding, so Dad sent his friend Gigi, a coworker, to pick me up. During the ride home, Gigi told me it meant a lot to Dad that I was coming home for the wedding. She said she and my father had a long conversation a few nights before and he asked her if she thought he was going to go to hell for what he'd done. I'm not sure if he was thinking about the divorce and impending remarriage outside of the Catholic Church, the infidelity and abuse, what he'd done in Vietnam, or something else. Maybe it was all of it. Whatever the case, he still had a conscience from his Catholic upbringing and knew he'd done things in the eyes of The Church that could potentially deny him a trip to heaven.

Despite her differences with our Dad, my sister lived in town and surprisingly chose to attend the wedding. I say surprisingly because, as noted earlier, she had seen, heard, and remembered much more than me. Plus, being a woman, she empathized with Mom and therefore was not on good terms with Dad. I decided to attend mostly because I'd learned to not rock the boat as I observed the battle of wills between Carey and Dad. Perhaps I unknowingly inherited that from Dad because, as noted earlier, he learned to play the game of staying out of the line of fire as he observed the interaction between his brother Corny and their father. I actually ended up having a good time and got to see my grandmother Helene and uncle Bud, her brother. About the wedding I wrote in my journal, *"I'm glad I went because Dad seemed very happy that I came."*

After the wedding, Carey grew in her ability to accept the relationship and started spending time with Dad and Jo. With divorce can come quite a few relational problems, one of which can be dealing with stepparents. That was never an issue with Jo because she always treated us with kindness and respect and never uttered a bad word about our mom. Unfortunately, Dad was transferred to Chicago within a year. That was hugely disappointing for Carey. As a child and young woman, she had a poor relationship with Dad. Just as their relationship seemed to be improving, the rug was pulled out from under her.

Another example of their contentious relationship occurred several years later in Chicago. Carey and Chris [sic: her husband of 35+ years as of the writing of this book] were in an established, committed relationship. Dad said they couldn't sleep together in the same bedroom. Carey couldn't accept that because she and Chris shared an apartment. But more than that, my Dad had lived with Jo for years before they finally married—while he was still married to our mother. Carey recognized the hypocrisy and called him out on it. The blow-up that ensued led to silence between them for six or seven years. It was during those years that Carey and Chris were married. Dad was not invited to the wedding, so I walked her down the aisle.

That was a real time of turmoil for our family. Whatever impact those events had on Carey, for better or worse, were obvious in her emotional comments about my dad at his funeral:

"When someone passes, especially a parent, we're left to ponder the legacy they leave us. My relationship with my father was neither easy nor close. In my younger years, I typically chose opposition to my father. We then passed through a long stretch of estrangement. And in the last few decades we emerged from the storm to find peace with our relationship by finally accepting each other for who we both were. Jo asked If I had pictures to include in the PowerPoint today. I brought out the old photo albums that I hadn't looked at in years. As I flipped through the albums, it was a recap of my early life. I reveled in seeing pictures of my mother and brother, grandparents, aunts, and uncles. But I was struck by the lack of pictures I have of my father.

In a way it made sense because I felt like my father wasn't around much growing up. My parents' marriage was not a good one and they were separated for many of the 20 years they were married. This was often a time of opposition between us. In some ways, I was my father's daughter. I was strong willed and didn't like being told what to do. A lyric from Bruce Springsteen's *Growin' Up* always rang true with me during this time.

> I hid in the clouded wrath of the crowd
> But when they said, 'Sit down,' I stood up
> Ooh, ooh, growin' up

In high school I realized that I didn't like the way my father treated me or my mother. Family may be given some latitude on how they deal with others in the family, but there comes a point when one says enough is enough for one's own well-being. If I wouldn't let other people treat me like that, why should my father? This led to a growing estrangement between us.

We didn't see each other or speak with one another much during this period. I didn't invite him to my wedding; rather, my brother Brian gave me away. It was during this time that I had clarity of thought and realized that I deserved better, but neither of us could change the other. It was just best to pursue the positive things in my life.

It wasn't until Brian and Jane had Abigail in 1995 that we both began to repair our relationship. I knew I wanted to be a part of Abigail's life. That meant I would no doubt see my father, who also wanted to be a part of her life. I'm not sure why, but as a gift I gave him a picture from my wedding. Jo told me he cried when he received it and said that it was the best gift he could have received. I think we both were ready to try to accept and respect each other.

My husband Chris and I had a child a few years later, Caleb. We had relocated to Arizona and my father was living in Florida. It was important that my father get to know my son as best as he could despite the distance. We traveled with some regularity to Florida to visit with Dad and Jo as well as other family in the state. Ours was never a deep relationship, more just below the surface, but we enjoyed the time we spent together and talked when apart.

More recently we were drawn closer together by a shared love of family history. I think that sense of the Ahearn family was always there, but since my father's heart procedure, he shared more about his family and growing up. I learned more about my father, and I felt more connected to him after these talks. He became less of a stranger to me.

I often turn to Kahlil Gibran's The Prophet in times of joy and sorrow. I find it helps center me. I reread "On Death" but it was "*On Love*" that spoke to me.

Then said Almitra, Speak to us of Love.

And he raised his head and looked upon the people, and there fell a stillness upon them. And with a great voice he said:

When love beckons to you, follow him,
Though his ways are hard and steep.
And when his wings enfold you yield to him,
Though the sword hidden among his pinions may wound you.
And when he speaks to you, believe in him,
Though his voice may shatter your dreams as the north wind lays waste the garden.

For even as love crowns you so shall he crucify you. Even as he is for your growth, so is he for your pruning.

Even as he ascends to your height and caresses your tenderest branches that quiver in the sun,

So shall he descend to your roots and shake them in their clinging to the earth.

I think it sums up my relationship with my father. In love there are good times and bad times. If it weren't for the bitterness, how would we know the sweetness? My roots may have been shaken throughout my life, but I still managed to flourish. I'm grateful that my father was able to see that and that we could forge a relationship that will remain with me, one that I can find comfort in now that he is gone.

So, the legacy my father leaves me is a confident sense of self. The branches that emerged from the shaken roots learned to sway in the breeze but not break."

As you may have guessed from Carey's comments, she and Dad eventually reconciled. She mentioned sending him the photo of her and Chris from the wedding. Dad's tears upon receiving the photo and comment that it was one of the best gifts he'd ever received, speak volumes.

When it came to family dynamics and drama, I didn't take sides. I got along with Dad, Mom, and Carey, whenever I was with them, and I never badmouthed any of them in conversation. I didn't enjoy confrontation, so I became a peacekeeper.

My college experience was even better than I could have imagined. I lifted weights, studied, and had fun on the weekends. As was the case during most of my life, I had a great group of friends. I was president of the Miami University Weightlifting Club for three years, which was a big responsibility because we had more than 200 members and a large budget. Between running the club and my major, I was setting myself up nicely to fulfill my dream of owning a gym. During college I went from 190 to 240 pounds, bench pressing 400 and squatting 600 pounds.

I worked just as hard in the classroom as I did in the gym. I set a goal to graduate Cum Laude and achieved it. I remember Dad telling me before going off to college—treat school like a job. Take your classes and study from eight a.m. to five p.m., then you can have as much fun as you want to at night and on the weekends. He was right. That disciplined approach worked like a charm. I got schoolwork out of the way by dinner so most nights I was in the gym for a couple of hours. I never pulled all-nighters. In fact, I can't remember ever studying past ten p.m. During finals weeks I would set an alarm, studying for 45 minutes then taking a 15-minute break every hour. I did that from eight a.m. till eight p.m. with hour-long breaks for lunch and dinner. It was amazing how quickly the days flew by using that approach. I was fortunate that the discipline I learned from sports and Dad helped so much in college and beyond.

During my sophomore year, Mom remarried. Time at home, summers in particular, were uncomfortable for me once she and her husband Don moved into their new place in the Columbus area. My sister still lived with them for a while when she attended the Ohio State University. Don didn't like having me around. I think he was jealous that Mom gave me lots of time and attention whenever I came home. An example of my discomfort was sleeping on a fold out metal cot that first summer they were in their new place. Nothing makes you feel more unwelcome than not having a real bed to sleep in all summer.

Another uncomfortable moment came when Don, a U.S. Marshall at the time, told me, "*I don't care if you're your mother's son. If I ever catch you with drugs, I'll bust your a***." Don was a gangly, kind of goofy looking guy who liked to believe he was Dirty Harry or some other super cop. He compensated for whatever he lacked by owning the biggest barrel gun he could find. I don't remember what I might have said in response to his comment but I'm pretty sure I was thinking, "*You're such a jerk!*"

For all of my Dad's missteps, one thing he and Mom drilled into me was that recreational drugs were wrong and dangerous. To this day I've never smoked a joint. I had plenty of friends who did that, and more, growing up and many more in college. They offered but I always declined. I never felt awkward saying no. Peer pressure in those situations wasn't an issue for me. Doing drugs just wasn't me and my friends respected me for it. When Jane met me, she said I was like a Boy Scout compared to the people she'd dated. I still take pride in that, sticking to who I am and what I believe. I don't try to impose my beliefs on anyone, but I'm pretty uncompromising on what I believe is right and wrong and have no problem sharing my beliefs if asked.

Like nearly every kid at college, I drank and had more than my share of times when I had too much to drink. One of those times led to an arrest for public intoxication and public urination my sophomore year. That cost me $150, which was a lot when the minimum wage was only $3.10 an hour! I'm not sure how my grandmother found out, but she wrote me a nice letter and sent me $5 for pizza. Her kindness and understanding surprised my Dad, but I think she knew I was an angel compared to him during his college days. One example of Dad's rowdiness came just before college graduation. He got into a bar fight with some buddies. The owner of the establishment went to the school and demanded that he not be allowed to graduate unless he and the others paid for the damage. The school agreed and it cost my grandmother $500 to see him walk across the stage in his cap and gown. That was quite a bit of money in 1962, the equivalent of about $5000 today!

I wrote that I never did recreational drugs, but to say I never took drugs would be misleading. I started taking steroids my senior year of college and did so for about five years. I was competing in powerlifting and wanted to try bodybuilding after I graduated. I rationalized that I wasn't doing drugs to escape anything and wasn't potentially endangering anyone by losing my faculties. I'd convinced myself that I was working hard pursuing a goal. On top of that, just about everyone else in the gyms where I lifted were doing the same. While all of that was true, it was still illegal, potentially dangerous, and wrong. I loved the years that I competed, but given a mulligan, I would make a different choice. I've learned that often what seems so important in the moment at different times in life usually turns out to not be nearly as important as we imagined. Time and experience are good teachers if we're willing to be students.

As I got ready to graduate from college, Mom's second marriage was about to end. To her credit, she thought she might have a drinking problem and stopped cold turkey. She really enjoyed her wine but hasn't had a drop in nearly 40 years. Don still wanted to go out to party with friends and didn't like that she'd given up that lifestyle. There were other dynamics at play too, and the marriage ended shortly after I graduated. I respect the fact that my Mom was unwilling to compromise on the drinking.

Starting My Career

I began my insurance career with The Travelers Insurance Company in July 1986. Before graduation I'd already accepted a retail job that would take me to Akron, Ohio, but the last week of school I got a letter from The Travelers. I knew nothing about insurance but thought I should look into the position because it was in Columbus. If I got the job, I'd be around family, friends, and the girl I'd been dating since high school. The girl was Janis, and she was living with my sister at the time. Because of mom's situation, I moved in with Janis's parents after college until I could find a place of my own.

The irony of the whole situation was that on the first day of work I met Jane. We both started in the underwriting trainee program. A few weeks later I was no longer going out with Janis. Jane and I hooked up one night after partying with friends. I felt guilty and told Janis the next day. It was almost like a divorce. We'd gone out so long and, because she was with my sister and I was at her parents' place, it was incredibly awkward. We both moved—her back home and I moved in with my sister for a few weeks until I could find an apartment. How the relationship ended with Janis and started with Jane is one of my biggest regrets in life. I definitely made the right choice to spend my life with Jane, but I wish I would have broken it off with Janis before going out with Jane. Despite Dad's flaws, he and Mom raised me with a strong sense of right and wrong, good and bad, so breaking up beforehand would have been the honorable thing to do.

Regarding cheating on Janis, I remember thinking, "I'm just like Dad," and it wasn't a proud feeling. It was a Cat's in the Cradle moment. Cat's in the Cradle is a song by Harry Chapin that begins with a father who's too busy to spend time with his young son. The son says, "One day, I'm gonna be like you, Dad." The song ends with the grown son telling the now elderly father he just doesn't have time to spend with him. The father realizes that indeed his son has grown up to be just like him. The song is a real tear-jerker.

If there's anything good that came from the ordeal with Janis and Jane, it's this—I learned from what happened and have been faithful in my marriage. Given the rates of infidelity and divorce, I'm proud of that. And, despite my anger issues early on, unlike Dad, I've never raised my hand in anger at Jane.

During my time with The Travelers, I was competing in bodybuilding. I loved everything about it—being in the gym, weights, dieting, the camaraderie, all of it. I recall Debbie Smith, the person responsible for my insurance training, asking me how "training" was going. I was getting ready for my first bodybuilding contest, so I started telling her all about what I was doing in the gym and my diet. When I paused, she interjected, "I'm talking about work." For me "training" was what you did in the gym, not something you did at work.

Although I was competing, somewhere along the way I let go of the dream of owning a gym. Life just happened—career, marriage, buying a home, etc. It wasn't until some 20 years later that I realized I'd fulfilled my dream. For decades I've had a great gym in my basement. I learned from that too and often tell people, sometimes we fulfill our dreams, but because it's not how we envisioned it we miss it. I'd been living my dream for many years before I realized it. As of the writing of this, every day for more than 30 years I've descended into my basement and done something I've loved since I was a teenager. That's one of the many blessings in my life.

When it came to my career, I spent the entirety of it in the insurance industry until I left to start my own speaking and consulting business in 2018. I knew nothing about the industry prior to getting into it but came to realize as insurance professionals we did two very noble things.

First, the insurance industry helps people. If insurance professionals do their jobs well, when tragedy strikes and people are properly covered, we help them get back on their feet. I remember explaining what I did to Abigail when she was young. I said, *"Did you see the tornado on tv today?"* She nodded and I told her, *"If those people have their insurance with my company, we are going to fix their cars, rebuild their homes, and all the kids will get their toys back."* At eight years old she understood what we did, we helped people.

The second thing insurance does is help the economy. No bank will loan tens of thousands, hundreds of thousands, or millions of dollars to buy homes, cars, and start or expand businesses, if you can't guarantee repayment should tragedy strike. When the insurance industry makes that guarantee there's a ripple effect throughout the economy as more cars are sold, homes are built, and businesses are started.

I still work extensively with insurance companies and agencies in my consulting because I'm proud to be a part of an industry that does those two very important things.

Marriage

After a somewhat on again, off again dating period, Jane and I were married on March 12, 1988. The rocky dating period was due to my indecision, which started when Janis, my ex-girlfriend, called in November 1986. That phone call threw me for a loop, and suddenly I didn't know who I wanted to be with. I was back and forth between Jane and Janis for about six months. I didn't want to hurt either person, but that's exactly and all that I did as I bounced back and forth between them during that time. The good news was, once I made up my mind I never looked back, never doubted the decision, never wondered, *"What if..."*, concerning the decision to marry Jane. The ability to make a choice then keep looking straight ahead has served me well throughout my life. I attribute much of that to Dad. Other than his advice about approaching school like a business, we never talked about how discipline would help me in life. Rather, I observed that he was dedicated to his career and disciplined in his approach to many things, like bettering his golf game. In addition, the discipline I received as a child stuck with me.

In early 1990 Jane moved on from The Travelers to CNA Insurance when The Travelers went through a reorganization in the sales and marketing department. On the heels of that we bought a home, and settled in Westerville, Ohio, a suburb north of Columbus. Within a few months of the move, I too left The Travelers and joined State Auto Insurance. That's a lot of change to take place in a three-month period!

The Power of Second Chances

The following year Dad turned 50. He was still living in Chicago and Jo threw him a surprise birthday party. That morning he and I played a round of golf. It was just the two of us because Jo and Jane were getting things squared away for the party. During that round I used Dad's old Ping knock off clubs because he was trying out a new set. At the end of the round, he gave me his old clubs. Even with all the advances in golf technology they're still the clubs I use when I play on occasion because it meant a lot coming from him on that special day. I didn't have a lot of father-son days like that so those clubs will always be special. The party was great, and I always think of Dad when I hear Louis Armstrong's *What a Wonderful World* because it's the song Jo played for the slide show commemorating his first 50 trips around the sun.

Dad's relationship with Jo is quite interesting and puzzling, considering how he mistreated my mom through the years. Jo's and Dad's relationship seemed to have affection and thoughtfulness that Mom and Dad's marriage lacked. Jo often said he was the most romantic man she'd ever met. Maybe there was something about Jo, or maybe Dad matured greatly over the years, or maybe it was a combination of the two, but Jo's and Dad's relationship was one of mutual affection and respect. This excerpt from some of Dad's writings is an example of his appreciation of her:

"Once while with friends, I was asked the most significant thing I had ever done in my life. My answer was quick and to the point, *'Being a Marine and leading men in combat!'* My wife Jo, whom I dearly love, looked sad. I then said, *'Marrying you was the second best.'*

I owe much to Jo. When I met her in 1979, I had been out of Nam for almost 13 years. She is the first and only person with whom I have shared some deep feelings about my experiences in Nam. She has been a pillar of strength, without whom I would be lost.

Up until I met Jo, I avoided all formal contacts with formal Marine functions. It was too difficult. With her help, I was able to visit The Wall for the first time. It was crushing to see the names of friends lost in Vietnam. As do most, I wept. It was a catharsis for me. She stood by me when I walked in a Chicago parade of Marines celebrating service in Vietnam; she was with me at the reunion of The First Marines in Indianapolis; she was with me at the Marine Corps Ball in Washington, D.C.; she encouraged me to help in honoring the Fallen Heroes of Florida. As she once said, I am her *'Rubberneck.'* To her I say, 'Thank you for bringing me back.'"

Despite all that had gone on between Mom and Dad, I was still proud to be his son and proud of him. He was

incredibly smart, successful in his career, still fit and athletic, and very good at anything he set out to do. When I was
young, I looked up to him so much that I wondered why he
didn't run for president. He always had answers and seemed
in charge no matter where we were or what we did. Despite
all of my admiration, things were about to take a dramatic
turn in our relationship.

A Phone Call Changes Everything

Life moved along and like many married couples, we
experienced our share of difficulties. We were just 23 years
old when we got married and both had a lot of growing up to
do when it came to loving each other and communicating with
honesty. By the grace of God, we got more deeply involved
with church, had a wonderful set of friends, and were able
to deal with our issues. During that time, I had a life changing event, similar to the Apostle Paul's encounter with Christ
on the road to Damascus. It was in the midst of our marital
struggles that I cried out, *"God, I don't care what you do with
Jane. Things have to be right between me and You."* It was
as if God said at that moment, *"Now I can work with you!"*
That's the day my relationship with God changed and as a
result, I went through dramatic personal changes. During that
same period Jane was changing too and to say that each of our
lives, and our marriage, were radically transformed would be
an understatement. Things were also about to change radically between me and Dad.

Neither Jane nor I grew up in particularly religious homes, but even as a child I had a deep sense that God existed. I attended church sporadically during college and after graduation, so when Jane and I started dating I asked her to join me. Years later she said inviting her to church stood out as something very different about me versus other guys she had dated.

My 30th birthday was on Good Friday, 1994. Jane was talking with Jo about Dad and Jo coming down to celebrate my birthday then spending the weekend with us so we could all go to Easter service. We were excited to show them our church and introduce them to some of our friends. Given Dad's Catholic upbringing, I thought Easter would be a non-threatening time for them to join us. Jo said Dad probably wouldn't want to go, and she and Jane decided it would be best if Dad and I talked about it rather than having the two women mediate it or just spring it on Dad.

The next day he called me and said they would come down from Mansfield, about an hour away, for my birthday, but would head home that night. I asked if he would spend the weekend with us then go to church. He said no. When I asked why, he said he just didn't want to go to church. I pressed him, asking why he didn't want to, and he insisted there was no reason, he just didn't want to. The conversation was getting uncomfortable, so he conveniently told me he was calling from an airport and had to catch his flight. He said if I wanted to talk, I could call him when he got home from his trip. I don't think he thought I'd follow up, but I did.

During that second phone call I pressed him about why he wouldn't go to church. It didn't seem like a big ask given that it was my 30th birthday and Easter weekend. He continued to insist he had no reasons; he just didn't want to go.

I said, "Dad, if we can't talk about your reasons, how can we talk about anything else?"

He told me, "We can talk about whatever you want to. I just don't want to go." As the conversation progressed, he slipped and said, "I have my reasons," to which I replied, "What are they?"

As I noted earlier, the Marine didn't like to be pressed or questioned. What came next shocked me. He blurted out, "Look, I know more about G**d*mn*d religion than you'll know in your whole f***ing life, and I don't care what you or anyone else says. I'm not a bad person!"

I replied, "Dad, I've never called you a bad person."

He followed with, "Oh yes you have, in so many words."

As we struggled to talk, he said, "Look, I don't like the way this conversation is going."

I came back with, "Dad, that's another thing we need to talk about. Life doesn't always go the way you want." Click... he hung up on me!

I wish Dad would have been willing to have genuine conversations about his faith, but he never wanted to go there. I didn't have enough life experience or perspective back then so I could only imagine why. Some would characterize his belief system as foxhole faith, from the old saying, "There are no atheists in foxholes." With Dad, there seemed to be the seeds of faith, but like most other things, he wanted matters of religion to be on his terms. Here is an excerpt from what he wrote about the twenty-third Psalm:

> "Thoughts of Vietnam came back a short while ago when I participated in reading The Bible in 90 Days. While reading Psalms, I came to Psalm 23 (ESV®):
>
>> 'The Lord is my shepherd, I shall not want.
>> He makes me lie down in green pastures;
>> He leads me beside quiet waters.
>> He restores my soul;
>> He guides me in the paths of righteousness
>> For His name's sake.
>> Even though I walk through the valley of the shadow of death,
>> I fear no evil, for You are with me;
>> Your rod and Your staff, they comfort me.
>> You prepare a table before me in the presence of my enemies;
>> You have anointed my head with oil;
>> My cup overflows.
>> Surely goodness and lovingkindness will follow me all the days of my life,
>> And I will [h]dwell in the house of the Lord forever.'

Our chaplains always recited this Psalm before
a big operation. Someone was on my side."

When Dad hung up on me, at that moment, it was as if
all the things I knew about what had happened between him
and Mom fell from my head to my heart. I was practically in
a rage! All I wanted to do was get in my car, make the hour
drive to his house, and physically tear him apart. At 53 years
old he might have still kicked my butt even though I was
much bigger and stronger than he was. Thankfully I called
Mom, and she talked me off of the proverbial ledge. Since
the divorce, she had encouraged Carey and me to maintain
relationships with Dad despite all that had transpired. However, once we began to do that later in life, mom's anger and
unforgiveness would become very apparent. Her reactions to
anything having to do with Dad and Jo made life for me, Jane,
and Abigail, extremely uncomfortable at times.

Regarding the phone call, that's the day everything
changed between me and my father.

Now it's Complicated

Once the veil is pulled away and truth is exposed, you can't
ignore it; otherwise, you're living in denial. I could no longer
get together with Dad, have a couple of beers, play some golf,
tell a few jokes, and act like everything was cool. Years before,
I'd told Janis right away about what happened between me
and Jane because I didn't want to live a lie. I took the same

approach with Dad because suddenly I started to have feelings about everything that had taken place in our family as I was growing up. I had questions and I wanted answers.

He and I decided to meet for dinner a few months after the blow up to try to hash things out. He couldn't understand why I wanted to revisit the past so I asked, "Dad, what would you do if I hit Jo?"

He leaned across the table, with all of his anger and intensity, staring me in the eye and said, "If you ever touch her, I'll f***ing kill you!" It was the same response he'd had with his father concerning the abuse his dad was directing towards my grandmother.

Then I said, "What if you found out it was five years ago?"

He replied, "I don't care when it was. If I ever find out you touched her, I'll f***ing kill you!"

That's when I said, "Good. Now you know how I feel about the divorce. I don't care that it was 12 years ago. For me it's right now and I want to talk about it." I'm not sure he truly understood, and we struggled during that conversation because most of his answers were surface level responses to hard questions. For someone who was so smart, he wasn't one to think deeply about who he was and why he did what he did. For example, I asked why he cheated on Mom and his reply was, "We didn't have enough sex." I knew that wasn't true. There was no exploration of any part of his past, family dynamics, the war, or anything else. As noted earlier in the quote from Ben Franklin, "There are three things extremely hard; steel, a diamond, and to know one's self."

At one point he said if he had it to do all over, he wouldn't change a thing because he was happy with who he was. That floored me! I questioned whether cheating on Mom and hitting her were necessary to become who he was. He'd not apologized to her and never did for the rest of his life. To this day, my mom still harbors much bitterness, resentment, and anger towards Dad. I don't know if an apology would have changed anything for her. Nonetheless, her unforgiveness is a trap she's been unable to escape, and it's affected all of her relationships to this day.

I don't remember much more about that day except to say that it was intense. Truthfully, I didn't know how he would respond, verbally or physically, to my questions, but I didn't care. The questions were consuming me, and he held most of the answers. Unlike my sister who cut him off for years, Dad and I remained on speaking terms and continued to see each other with some regularity. However, it was difficult because I couldn't enjoy a round of golf, a couple of beers, and a nice dinner like I had in the past. I felt there was always an elephant in the room, important issues that needed to be addressed.

As a quick side note, many years after I'd been married, I called my old girlfriend Janis to apologize for how things ended. As I write this and reflect on so many things, I'm glad I didn't let history repeat itself. We can't take back our actions but acknowledging how you've hurt someone and saying you're sorry can be a big step in the healing process for the person who was hurt.

Despite many attempts at having children, Jane and I had trouble conceiving. Then, in 1994, Jane had a tubal pregnancy that required the removal of one of her fallopian tubes. At that point we knew conventional attempts to get pregnant were out the door for us, so we started to consider adoption. On the advice of a couple of doctor friends who were in a Bible study with us, we decided to give in vitro-fertilization a try. Our second attempt worked! On December 6, 1995, our daughter Abigail entered the picture.

Abigail's birth had a huge impact on our family. While she was the 11th grandchild for Jane's family, she was the first grandchild on my side of the family. Mom was great during the pregnancy, always giving Jane a small gift every time she saw her during those nine months. We thought the best gift we could give Mom and Carey would be to have them present for the delivery. Seeing Jane give birth changed my sister's thinking about having a child of her own. That resulted in Carey and Chris having Caleb just over two years later. Abigail's arrival also meant there might be times when my parents would cross paths.

Coming into the world by in vitro fertilization wasn't normal so Jane and I wondered how we would tell Abigail. When Abigail was 12 years old Jane told her about the circumstances surrounding her birth. The next day Jane was off doing something, and Abigail and I were having dinner, so I decided to ask her what she thought about it. She responded like many kids her age would and said, *"Nothing."* I told her, *"You know what's really cool, you're just like Jesus."*

She asked why and I replied, "*Mom and Dad didn't have to have sex to have you. How many of your friends can say that?*" Knowing kids think it's gross to imagine their parents having sex, suddenly her birth by in vitro was a badge of honor for Abigail!

As I just noted, Abigail coming into the world meant there might be times when my parents would cross paths. I soon discovered that contrary to what some people believe, divorce does not end all problems, especially when children are involved. There are just new problems that emerge and develop over time. The consequences of a bad divorce reared their ugly head in November 1996, resulting in another intense conversation with Dad.

Abigail's first birthday was approaching, and we asked if he and Jo would come down for the party. He said they couldn't because of his work. That allowed us to extend an invitation to Mom without her worrying about him being there. The anger and hurt from his infidelity and abuse, and the divorce were starting to rear its ugly head with Mom at any thought of encountering him. For example, thinking Dad and Jo might be present for Abigail's baptism, Mom refused to come to the ceremony or the gathering we'd planned for friends and family afterwards. I was having to play mediator which was a lingering consequence of a bad divorce.

Regarding the birthday party, I was in South Carolina for work when Jane called and said she'd had a conversation with Dad, and he'd gotten nasty because of the birthday party situation. Apparently, his plans changed so he wanted to come down. I called him and he was his usual jovial self to start. He told me his plans changed and that he and Jo would come down for the birthday celebration. I let him know he couldn't, and he asked why. I told him once he said they couldn't come, we'd invited Mom and she couldn't be around him. His jovial tone disappeared, and he said, *"When are you going to grow up and make a f***ing decision!?"*

How could he in all seriousness ask me that question? I'd made major decisions all my life. Professionally, I train other leaders how to make tough, but good decisions. Where was Dad's question coming from? Why did my decision light such a fuse in him? I replied, *"I am making a decision. You're not coming."* And that was that.

Now I understand much more about what was really happening during that exchange, and many others, between Dad and myself. If you consider all I've shared about him, you can see why that set him off. He was used to getting his way, but I wasn't budging because it would have been unfair to Mom, and I felt she'd been through enough.

Perhaps Dad perceived my response as indecisiveness—having invited him, then telling him he could not attend—as weakness and passivity, character traits that will get people killed on the battlefield. In the military, especially in combat, decisions have to be made in the amount of time it takes to snap your fingers. Decisions that are made in a matter of seconds may have life altering consequences. Time to deliberate, ask for lots of input, and let research marinate is preferable, but that's not always possible.

My father related such an occasion, when he had to make a critical decision in a matter of moments. As you read the account in his own words, you'll better understand his challenge to me, which I interpreted as demeaning, to *"make a decision."*

"My platoon was sent out on a long-range recon patrol. About two days out, we were hit by a large group of VC (Viet Cong) near a local village. The platoon regrouped in a cemetery for better cover. We were surrounded and needed air support quickly. I didn't have an ALO (Artillery Liaison Officer) with the platoon and because of the proximity of the VC and their size, I called in an airstrike near our front lines. It was only partially effective, and I called in a second strike. That routed the VC, but it wounded two of my Marines. We were soon airlifted back to base camp."

So, as you can see, my father's decision was based on the goal of saving an entire platoon of Marines. To him, a decision about who could attend a child's birthday party, was indeed child's play, if you'll pardon the pun.

A fellow Marine of my father's, Tom Vanderzyl, reached out to our family when he received news of Dad's passing. Tom's comments are also included later in the Family and Friends section. Tom's description is in many ways a metaphor for Dad's life.

> "I saw (your father) our Skipper being blown up and flying through the air with four other guys. He picked himself up, dusted himself off, saluted and headed up the hill as did Corporal Paskoski (who got a Purple Heart) ...we had an in-depth email conversation about that day. He was one of our finest Marines."

Did you see it? He picked himself up, dusted himself off, saluted and headed up the hill. That was my dad, the man I'm proud of.

Another factor in how quickly our conversation escalated could have been an impression by Dad that I was being disloyal to him. Faithfulness and loyalty go hand-in-hand as core values for a Marine. Semper Fi. I believe my father misinterpreted my thoughtfulness and empathy toward my mother as disloyalty to him. To a Marine, disloyalty is absolutely unacceptable.

Take a look at how my dad describes the loyalty of Captain Keenan, when a Major challenged my father's decision to call in the airstrike.

> "After returning to base camp, there was an inquiry because of the wounded Marines. A fat

a**ed Major from Danang came to Hill 41 and told my CO (Commanding Officer), Capt. Keenan, that he wanted to talk to the lieutenant who miscalled the airstrike. The Major was a jerk and started to really get on me, saying I didn't know my position and caused the mishap. After a few minutes, Capt. Keenan interjected, saying that I was one of his best officers and trained in airborne terrain appreciation. After about three minutes, he literally threw the Major off the hill, and we never heard from them again. I knew Keenan from Hawaii, where I served as one of his platoon commanders. He was responsible for me getting promoted to Battalion staff even as a relatively junior officer. A real Marine."

"A real Marine" is how my father described the man who showed loyalty to him. The other individual? The one who questioned my father's judgment? Well, he got what he deserved, didn't he?

When I gave my father's eulogy, I shared that if he were still with us, I'd tell him, *"Dad, like you, I'm a warrior. I didn't fight for our country, I fought for something more important...I fought for you and me. I was willing to put up with the intensity of your anger and unwillingness to talk at times in order to have a closer, deeper relationship with you. I wanted to learn things that would help me understand you and help me be a better son, a better husband, and a better father."*

I believe one more contributing factor to our altercation was that things were not going well for him at work.
He wanted to be president of the company he was with,
and it wasn't going to happen. I think losing control there
and not being able to control things with me were hard on
the Marine who was used to giving orders. Later in life I
empathized with what was happening with him because I
left State Auto Insurance under similar circumstances. He
ended up taking early retirement the next year and moved
to Florida shortly thereafter.

Several years ago, Jane and I were out one night with
someone she played golf with regularly. Joseph served in The
Marines in the early 1970s and was a little younger than Dad.
Like Dad, Joseph was also divorced and remarried. We were
sitting at a bar when the issue of Marines and their kids came
up. Joseph said his kids questioned him on things from his
past and he told them whatever he'd done was none of their
business. I got angry and said, loud enough for people around
us to hear, "Bullsh**! Your choices impacted them." I think
he was taken aback by my intensity, but I wasn't going to let
that lie persist. How could I when I was coming to realize how
my father's past impacted me?

These conversations are really hard, but the reality is,
what our parents say and do is a huge factor that shapes who
we are—good and bad. I hope you can see that with my father

and his family dynamics growing up in such a dysfunctional home. In my case, I wanted to know Dad better because he was my father and so I might understand myself more. I wanted to be the best husband, father, and friend I could be. I wanted to learn from Dad's mistakes and mine so our daughter Abigail would be better off. If each of us can look at our kids and honestly say they're better people than we are, that's a good thing! It's not a contest, it's about making the world a better place one person at a time. That's less likely to happen if we blindly repeat the same mistakes and I'd seen enough of that in our family history. Einstein put it well when he said, *"Insanity is doing the same thing over and over and expecting different results."* I wanted to stop the insanity for me and my family.

Things gradually began to get better between me and my father, but it was hard. Jane could see that I visibly changed whenever we were around him. One year he and Jo were with us for Christmas, and I realized I couldn't remember ever telling him that I loved him. I resolved to do that but felt bound up whenever I thought about saying it. Jane could see my nervousness. No time seemed like the right time to blurt out, *"I love you."* That's sad because you should be able to say that freely to the people you're closest to. It wasn't until we dropped them off at the airport that I finally worked up the courage to utter the words. There was no time left because he and Jo were in line at the ticket counter. It wasn't as emotional as I'd made it out to be in my mind. He responded with, "*I love you too.*" That first step made it easier to say it going forward.

There were still disappointments ahead. He didn't make it to Ohio for my 40th or 50th birthday celebrations. I never understood why he didn't do either. That would have meant a lot because we'd traveled to Chicago for his 50th, then to Florida for his 60th. Despite being disappointed, I was better equipped to deal with it. Jane was incredibly helpful. She's a naturally caring person who's easy to talk to because she's so inquisitive. Her caring nature was never more apparent than when Dad passed away. After my eulogy, I hugged her and cried like a baby for what seemed like an eternity. More than once I marveled at how Jane would lean into Jo's pain by asking her insightful questions. Jane cried with her, shared her own pain at Dad's passing, and encouraged Jo with scripture.

Whenever we went to Florida to visit it was apparent to me that Dad was genuinely happy to see us. We could tell by the smiles, the hugs, and the "*I love you*" exchanges when we arrived and left. I think those visits were more for him than for us.

A Different Man by the End

"Such were some of you; but you were washed, but you were sanctified, but you were justified in the name of the Lord Jesus Christ and in the Spirit of our God."
—1 Corinthians 6:11 (NASB®)

Fathers and Sons: It's Complicated

Despite Covid, when Dad died, Jane, Abigail, and I flew to Florida for the funeral service. I chose not to go down early to see him before he was cremated because I didn't want my final memory of seeing him to be a lifeless corpse. He was too big a personality to be remembered that way. My last interaction with him was when he texted me on September 2, 2020. I'd asked him about an old photo he'd tried emailing me and he wrote:

> "I am trying to clean up some very large files
> here at the house, so I am going through them

meticulously. That's how I found the picture. I know the picture you're talking about. If I come across it, I'll let you know. By the way I came across a letter you sent me on my 70th birthday. It was beautiful. It brought tears to my eyes. I have some younger friends 70-ish who are experiencing health problems that make mine look minor. I've been around for a long time and have had some wonderful experiences and memories. You and Carey are among them. Have a great day."

I'm so thankful for that final text. I'm even more thankful I wrote dad that letter. At the time I wrote it, I had no way of knowing how much it would mean to him. In the midst of some unpleasant memories with my dad, knowing my words brought some joy to him in his final days is gratifying to me. Here's my letter to Dad:

Dad,

Happy 70th birthday (4/22/11)! Because I'm fairly good at math I'm pretty sure this one only comes around once so enjoy it to the fullest. I know you're competitive so if life is a race, then every year that goes by gives you a better and better chance of winning. ;)

Sorry we are not there to celebrate with you but I'm glad we've been making it a point to spend some Christmases and vacations together in recent years. I got you the funny card, like always, but also wanted to take time to write you a note.

The more time goes by the more I appreciate what you did for me. I remember taking Jane to Miami University for my 10-year reunion and she was floored because it was so beautiful. I was too because it was even better than I remembered. Like many things in life, that time at college was special but I didn't fully appreciate it in the moment. Without anything to compare it to, it's hard. I try to teach Abigail to appreciate things in the moment because all too fast the moment is gone, and we look back and wish for just one more day. Thanks, because I am very fortunate to have gone to that school.

Speaking of school; had I not yielded to your advice about business it's very likely that I would not have worked for The Travelers, met Jane, and there would be no Abigail. What seemed like an insignificant decision was far bigger than I could have imagined.

I also remember you telling me to treat school like a business. Go to class and do my homework from 8 to 5, then I could do what I wanted with the rest of my time. I don't know if you knew it but that's what I did. School work was always done by dinner then the night was reserved for weightlifting.

I've made mistakes in my life, but I think more than most I had a strong sense of right and wrong. To this day I've never tried recreational drugs. Like all college kids I drank—thus the urination incident—but I steered clear of the potentially bad stuff even though many of my friends indulged. As I said, I had a pretty strong sense of right and wrong and I got that from you and mom.

The discipline I have towards all the things I do came mostly from you. When I tell people about me, something I mention early on is that I'm the son of a Marine. That explains an awful lot to them. My friends still tease me, and one said, "*We lifted weights, but you had to be a bodybuilder. We took up jogging, but you ran marathons. Now you get your black belt.*" Something you may not know but during the time when we were more involved in church as I read through The Bible, I began to put down my thoughts. The document ended up being a thousand pages. Whatever I did, I wanted to do it to the best of my ability, and I believe that came from you.

Something you shared about your Marine experience that stuck with me was the time the Vietnamese soldier was being kicked by the Vietnamese CO, trying to get info as he lay there dying. You said you pulled your gun on the CO to get him to stop then cradled the man till he died. Any time I share that with someone it would make me tear up just like it did as I typed this letter. Of all the things you've shared with me, that makes me proudest because that took unbelievable courage. To me that epitomizes what's at the core of you.

If I had something to do over in life, I think I would have chosen to be a Marine. I loved the camaraderie football gave us and that's why I'm such good friends with Russell, so many other high school buddies, and Coach Alles. There was something about being under the lights on Friday night with those other 10 guys that can't be explained. I'm sure basic training and combat multiplied that infinitely. When I see you meet other Marines, especially those who served in Vietnam, I sometimes think you're closer to them than you are to me. I'm not jealous, I admire it.

I'm happy for you that you and Jo have found so much happiness together. It's been nice to see you grow and change because of her. She's been good for you. And it's been wonderful that Jane loves you both too. That's something Jane and I have been blessed with—each having in-laws we really enjoy being with.

I'm sorry we had some rough times around my 30th birthday. Now that time has passed, I hope you can understand from your relationship with your own dad that I hit a period where I had questions and just wanted to understand things. I've tried to use mistakes you and Mom made to learn from. You once told me, "*I don't care what you or anyone else says, I'm not a bad person.*" I honestly never thought you were, so I apologize if I said or did things that made it seem that way.

As a kid I didn't dwell on what you and Mom were going through, I just immersed myself in football and Janis. But as I got older and tried to figure out why I was the way I was, I knew that period had a huge impact on me, so I wanted to get a handle on things. Again, I hope you can understand. Just so you know, I'm still trying to figure out a lot of things, but I feel I've mellowed in my approach.

So, while you're celebrating 70, we'll be in Chicago celebrating what I hope is a new chapter for me with blogging and speaking. The days in Chicago were good days when you lived there. What stands out to me was taking Jane to meet you then getting engaged. It was a great period so hopefully we can catch a little of that magic this weekend while you catch some with Jo and friends. We're looking forward to having you up this summer.

Love,
Breen

Less than two weeks after sending the heartfelt text Dad was gone. Maybe your relationship with a parent is complicated. If so, I hope this helps. Either way, if you can, give them a hug today. If not, I'm sure a phone call will be appreciated. There will come a day when you want to do one or the other but cannot. When I look back on the text from Dad, and some earlier emails he sent, it made me think, it's almost as if he knew his time was coming. In hindsight Jo noticed it too. She said she came home one day, and he was looking over old cards and letters they'd exchanged, and he told her how much he loved her. He never would/could have verbalized it, but his actions were like someone getting things in order before going away.

During our trip for his funeral, it was so nice to hear all the stories from friends and neighbors about the impact Dad had on them. One example was a young lady who'd lived across the street. She decided to go to college in her 30s while married and raising kids. No easy endeavor! She told us how my father helped her with papers she had to write. When I say helped, it wasn't that he wrote them. No, he questioned her about the topic, how she would present it, and made corrections. He did the same for me by often pointing out mistakes in my blog posts that needed to be corrected.

I'm not sure I fully appreciated the impact Dad had on others until I heard and read so many comments from people as news of his passing reached the concentric circle of family and friends. Here is a sample of the notes and kind words others expressed to us.

Tom Vanderzyl, Marine, Facebook post

The photograph on the right has been cropped and I believe some guys are sitting on the side of the hill in front of him (Brian Ahearn) ...I am one of them. The hill over the Skipper's left shoulder is Bravo Hill (B Co. 1/1/1 I-Corps 66). The Skipper and I started exchanging stories via email a few (God bless Al Gore for inventing the internet) years ago. I saw (your father) our Skipper being blown up and flying through the air with four other guys. He picked himself up, dusted himself off, saluted and headed up the hill as did Corporal Paskoski (who got a Purple Heart) ...we had an in-depth email conversation about that day. He was one of our finest Marines. RIP Skipper, the line has held.

Jim Caldwell, family friend

Hello Brian,

I just viewed the service. Beautiful! Rory shared a vivid story of your young father and the life of his family. I was especially moved by your words. Yes, fathers and sons, a great love that sometimes maybe often comes to bear between the two late in life. It did with me. Maybe only in faith after fathers depart. Your father told me over and over and over again how much he loved you and how proud he was of you. I imagine Brian's gun held at the head of that CO and an enemy dying in your father's comforting arms. He told you this story, I imagine, to reveal so many emotions twisted together, perhaps held in confinement. His love for you was somewhere there, as it was with that man. Your father was a great man and I think his son is too. Brilliant!

Please let Jane know that she did a terrific job delivering my words.

It was so good to see you even though by video. We wish we could have been there in person.

Brian, it hurts losing Brian, all his voices, his life, his thinking, and expressions. You inspired me to believe that all about losing Brian that hurts now will surely become joyful and loving memories. Thank you!

Sarah and I extend our sympathy for your loss and wish for love and peace for you, Jane, and your family.

Sincerely,

Jim

Bill Walton, Marine

Marines are not necessarily good at expressing our emotions. We have a bond, and our friends are really our friends. Brian was my non-blood brother, and I was part of the entire [sic: Ahearn] clan! I always (for some reason) would think of him when I read or heard this poem.

Under the wide and starry sky,
Dig the grave and let me lie.
Glad did I live and gladly die,
And I laid me down with a will.
This be the verse you grave for me:
Here he lies where he longed to be.
Home is the sailor, home from sea,
And the hunter home from the hill.
Semper Fi!

David Conway, friend

Brian's passing is a major loss to all of us. He was smart, funny, a great conversationalist, caring, dedicated to family, and someone who never met a stranger. The Yankee universe is emptier here and filled another seat in heaven. We will all miss you!

Megan Ahearn, sister-in-law

My heart and prayers go out to Jo, his kids, grandkids, and his pup Bella. Brian was a source of strength and many smiles I came to depend on. He simply cared about you and was always there for you. We shared the book on common sense and knowing right from wrong. I'll miss his morning emails, frequent calls, and funny texts. I'm so very grateful and blessed to have had this proud Marine touch my life and make it a happier one. I think he would have enjoyed that poem too.

Tom Sgritta, former coworker and friend

I'm shocked to hear about B.F.X. Brian was a real friend as well as a leader. He helped make my life and had a huge influence on what I did. For a year he was my boss, and a great one at that. But he has been a close friend for forty-two years. We saw each other often for much of that time. Lately most of our communication was by email, but we still felt close.

I learned a great deal from Brian. He taught me much about people, planning, logic, and enjoying life. Often, I tell stories of activities that involved both Brian and me. I will miss him much. My heart goes out to Jo and his family.

Barbara Cooley, wife of Marine Mike Cooley

Dear Breen,

This heartfelt letter to your dad has brought forth a barrage of tears just when I thought no more were there. My husband, Mike and I were blessed to know your father for almost twenty adventurous years! Mike is also a Vietnam Marine, and they shared that special bond the Brotherhood is based on. That and fishing!

The Captain's writings...he will always be the Captain to me...so eloquently done, will never be duplicated. No one has his wit and knowledge to make a point! Always accurate, always insightful. A very special man indeed, always there for whatever was needed. He leaves a hole in our lives never to be filled and he will be loved, always.

Mike and Barbara Cooley

P.S. I forgot to mention his restaurant quality short ribs! Another talent!

Ronald Falzarano, Marine

Brian,

You do not know me, but I was both a friend and Brother Marine to your dad. I did not know that he had passed, and I am so sorry for our loss. I am a Korean Vet, and we did share many stories, mostly about changes in The Corps. We also fished many bass tournaments together with the Lakeland Bassmasters where we met. It had been a long time since we met but kept in contact by email.

My deepest sympathy,

Ron

Megan Ahearn, sister-in-law

Dear Brian,

Thank you for sending me the beautiful video of your father's service. It was all so touching. The Marine tribute to him certainly made us all proud. I only wish I could have been there for all of you. Your father was the best, and I'll miss the relationship we built over the last few years. He had become an important part of my life, especially after Denis's [sic: Dad's brother] passing. He was as proud of you as you are of him. Please stay in touch and thank you so much again. Stay well, my prayers will be with you and your family.

Love,

Megan

Bill Walton, Marine

I have recently gone through a come to Jesus meeting with my son. He raised his voice at me and pretty much laid into me for a dispute he thought I had with his wife. We never had a bad word and he seemed to be saying I'm 55 years old and I'm my own man.

The old Marine in me came out just short of smacking him for disrespect. But I caught myself and pondered why fathers and sons seem to have these moments. I saw it with your uncles and other friends as well. Yet we all seem haunted by our relationship with our fathers? My dad was a traveling salesman with fair pay. We didn't have much but he always got food on the table and clothes on our backs. He never said, "I love you," embraced us, kissed us, he just took care of us.

I grew up and fathered similarly, providing, and working all the time. I never told my son I loved him until he was in his forties! I struggled with saying it because I thought I showed it. I did coach him in baseball up to high school and we had that. He marvels at the Marine bond, as the closest he came was college baseball buddies.

Your dad would tell me how good you were, and I would laud my kid's efforts, but we never shared our inner feelings about you guys. My son senses I may be getting close as he sees my slow pace, joint replacements, and the old man losing his strength. The end of the cycle. We as fathers who were affected by war years, protests when we got home, and evil, are not the same as many dads who were draft dodgers or joined the air national guard, or claimed they were gay. I hope you guys understand that. Your generation suffered with fathers who were in the fight, tried not to bring it home, and shut off the questions!

Brian was proud to be your dad! I wish you well.

Bill Walton, Marine

Very touching [sic: the blog post I wrote about fathers and sons]. All those functions I shared with your dad were laugh fests as we remembered the Marine days. Never the dark stuff, just the goofy things and whacky guys The Corps attracted. He was a captain which is one step down from God in the Marines. No General ever got there without commanding a company of grunts. I was a buck sergeant from Brooklyn. I enlisted to shake off the troublemakers I hung out with. I went

through three captains. Our ranks never allowed fraterniza-
tion, but they were good guys and listened when things got
hot. They relied heavily on the NCOs (Non-commissioned
Officers) and had our respect even though they would get
chicken sh** with petty stuff and we'd pass it on. "Sh** rolls
downhill" was our mantra to the privates!

So many things you encountered with him resonated with me.
Quick to bark and too tough to admit I'm wrong. I can't make the
funeral. We flew up to NJ to take care of some colleagues on my
community board whose wives are very sick. Two-week quaran-
tine before we could interact. I'm heading back on October 25.
We do all the vendor bidding oversee all maintenance. So, with
two out of four directors unable to function, I had to come back.
I hope you can pass on the good and avoid the bad as your kid's
progress! Thanks for being a good son ;)

Another story came from a pastor during the funeral. He
shared that Dad took his son Cooper fishing. Cooper caught a
catfish, so Dad nicknamed him Catfish Cooper and got him a
sweatshirt with his new nickname embroidered on it. I don't
know Cooper, but I have no doubt he will never forget Mr.
Brian who took him fishing.

While sitting outside late one night Jane, Abigail, and I
talked about the stories we were hearing. Jane asked me,
*"Does it bother you that he wasn't that way with you growing
up?"* There was a time when it would have, but with the passage of time and understanding I was able to honestly tell them
it didn't bother me. In fact, it made me happy. I think with age

comes more life experience, wisdom, hormones change (guys get less aggressive), and we contemplate life more as we see the finish line. In addition, as I wrote earlier, it's not how we start the race but how we finish. Dad grew as a person and changed. He was someone people truly enjoyed being around because he'd experienced so much as he traveled the world and served our country. He was full of great stories and still excelled at telling jokes. As my Uncle Rory mentioned at the funeral, when Dad entered a room, you knew it. He had a positive impact on many people and because of that they miss him. I hope my last days will be my best and that I will have a positive impact on people until the day I die. Or to put it another way, the best is yet to come. That was the case for Dad.

Dad and Abigail on a catch and release mission. He certainly loved her and I think being a grandparent gave him an opportunity to do things differently.

Upon Reflection

"Do not judge, so that you will not be judged. For in the way you judge, you will be judged; and by your standard of measure, it will be measured to you."
—Matthew 7:1-2 (NASB®)

Marines are Human

Despite the tough exterior, never forget that Marines are human. They're made of the same stuff you and I are made of—flesh and blood, full of sorrows and joys. This became clearer in the summer of 2020 when a group of friends and I decided to read *The Body Keeps the Score: Brain, Mind, and Body in the Healing of Trauma* by Bessel van der Kolk. As noted earlier, the book helped certain insights around PTSD drop from my head to my heart.

For example, I used to look at some works of art and think, *"Whoever made that must be whacked!"* Now I realize there's just no way for some people to put into words what's going on inside of them, but their art expresses what they're feeling and dealing with. The more I thought about that, and the more I imagined Dad in a firefight, seeing friends wounded, killed, or blown to pieces, the more I felt for him.

In the next section you'll read Dad's writings on his Vietnam experience. One of his stories always makes me tear up. In fact, whenever I share it with anyone, I cry. He not only wrote about it, but he also told me about it firsthand. When I shared it with his brother Kevin, he had no clue. Apparently, Dad wasn't talking to anyone about what went on in Vietnam except me, Jo, and some Marine friends.

Dad told me a Viet Cong soldier had been gut shot and it was clear he would die. The South Vietnamese commander was kicking the dying man, trying to get information from him. My father, an intelligence officer, was present. He said he couldn't take the brutality any longer, so he put his revolver to the commanding officer's head and said, *"I'll blow your f***ing brains out if you kick him again."* What chokes me up the most is he said the man died in his arms under a tree. For just a moment please imagine the courage it took to do that at 24 years old, thousands of miles from home.

That's the man I needed to know! Underneath all of my questions and anger, that's the man God was pushing me to know at a deeper level. That one story let me know that despite everything, Dad *had not* lost his moral compass. That's the man I'm proud to call my father. I now understand this about my father: *whoever* needed help, he would have stepped into the fray because he was a warrior and would do what was right. Would you stop one of your own from mistreating or killing someone who was the enemy? Remember, he'd seen his friends fall at the hands of those very same people. I pray should I ever find myself in a similar situation that I will have the courage he displayed in that moment. Knowing my father did it, knowing I possess his DNA, gives me confidence that I will be up to the task.

Recruiting day NYC, 1966. Dad is at the far right.

Separate the Good from the Bad

It's so easy to get distracted, and sometimes over-whelmed. As a result, because of the bad behavior you sometimes fail to see the good. I've spoken to many people whose fathers served in the Marines, and other branches of the military, and the stories are similar in many respects—strict discipline, don't talk back, do as I say, don't question me. That's to be expected given the command-and-control structure of the military where life and death are often on the line.

Unfortunately, too often the behaviors also include drinking, drugs, womanizing, verbal and, frighteningly, physical abuse. This is *not* to say all Marines do all of these. Absolutely not. But some do as they cope with military life. Throw on top of that the trauma of battle and you have a potent recipe for PTSD.

If you can get past what I've described, hopefully you can begin to see the good as I have. As I reflect, here are a handful of things I've learned from having a father who served and used much of his experience to raise me.

Discipline. Between my father and coaches, I came to appreciate the value of hard work and discipline: getting up early, the ability to focus, making myself sit and do whatever was necessary to succeed. These are results of the discipline Dad instilled in me.

Commitment. Over the years I've told people that I don't have a lot of interests; but, whatever I do, I want to do it to the best of my ability. Fear has never prevented me from trying an activity. I usually ask myself, *"Am I willing to commit to something so much that I do it well and enjoy it?"* If the answer is no, then I don't take it on.

Effort. On the heels of discipline and commitment is effort. I may be committed and possess discipline, but success still requires focused effort. As my old high school football coach, Todd Alles, a Navy vet, used to say, *"If you don't have time to do it right, when are you going to find time to do it over?"* Put in the effort to do it well so you have no regrets.

Fidelity. Semper Fi, always faithful, is the Marine Corps motto. In marriage Dad fell woefully short on his first try, but I believe he was faithful to Jo and treated her well. Somehow, she helped him overcome some of his demons from his time in The Corps and Vietnam. Once issues such as that are settled, it's easier to start becoming the person you were meant to be. I know Dad was loyal to the Marines and those who served in other branches of the military. I think my wife, daughter, and friends, would describe me as faithful and loyal.

Education. Dad set a standard that we were expected to do well in school. That goes back to his father and the value the Ahearn clan put on education. It's not that Dad was *"gifted"* and therefore smarter than others. On the contrary, his high school performance proved he wasn't. I certainly wasn't either. If I worked hard, I usually got As. Early in college I took one test lightly and got a D. That made me question whether or not I was cut out for college, and it caused me to work harder. I'm more thankful for that D than any other grade I received during college because of the positive impact it had on me.

Finishing. The ability to make a decision then following through has served me well throughout my life. I attribute much of that to Dad disciplining me as a child around the grass cutting incident. The Bible says in Hebrews 12:11, *"No discipline seems pleasant at the time, but painful. Later on, however, it produces a harvest of righteousness and peace for those who have been trained by it."* That pivotal lesson has paid huge dividends for me and has benefited others who had to rely on me. Dad's message was clear and has stuck with me: finish what you start.

Don't Judge

Jesus tells us, "*Do not judge, and you will not be judged. Do not condemn, and you will not be condemned. Forgive, and you will be forgiven.*" I don't think it's wrong to call out someone's actions when they're harmful. My father's infidelity and physical abuse directed at my mother was wrong. Nothing justifies it. The pain it caused Mom and the impact on me and my sister still lingers.

Having said that, I don't condemn my father. I wish he were alive to hear me say, "*I forgive you.*" I never had a chance to utter those words. I have no idea how I would have responded that day when he pulled his revolver on the South Vietnamese commanding officer who was brutalizing the dying man. I have no idea what life would be like growing up with an alcoholic father for whom I could never seem to measure up. I don't know what I would have done with the experiences Dad had in Vietnam. To assume "I know" is folly, wishful thinking. If the Apostle Peter could spend three years with Jesus, saw the miracles, professed with all his heart that he'd never forsake Him, only to deny Him three times, then who am I, and who are you, to "know" how we would respond in any situation?

It's right to confront bad behavior and tell someone, "What you're doing is not right. It's hurting you, me, and our family." If you try to understand what brought that person to where they are and remember, *"But for the grace of God, there go I,"* you will have more compassion for them. It could just be your love and compassion that turns them in a different direction. I wish I'd understood that sooner in life.

Parting Words of Wisdom

"He will turn the hearts of the fathers back
to their children and the hearts of the children
to their fathers, so that I will not come
and strike the land with complete destruction."
—Malachi 4:6 (NASB®)

D espite what transpired with Mom and Dad, then the struggles my father and I had, he was a different person by the end of his life. I used to be very prickish, a real jerk at times, and very selfish. I think those were lingering effects of growing up with the turmoil my sister and I experienced. But, by the grace of God I changed. By the same grace my father changed too. After the struggles we went through, our hearts were inclined to one another at the end. My encouragement to you my friend, is to never lose hope!

Marines

I've not walked in the shoes of a Marine, so I won't pontificate a list of things someone who has served needs to do. However, having been raised by a Marine, I think I can still offer some wisdom. When I use the word wisdom, here's what I mean: the application of knowledge.

If you're a Marine, I encourage you to seek professional help, even if you don't think you need it. And please don't ignore what's going on in the home. For example, my physical altercations with my sister in middle school and high school were not good or healthy. Fortunately, the violence never progressed for either of us afterwards. Admitting you need help before things fall apart isn't easy, but don't wait. For example, have you experienced any of the following?

- Outbursts of anger that are disproportionate responses to situations.
- Not talking about how you really feel.
- The desire to hurt yourself or others.
- Suicidal thoughts.
- Withdrawal from loved ones and activities you used to enjoy.

Even if you've not experienced some of what was just noted, why not take advantage of the opportunity to talk to a professional? Begin your journey of healing *before* you lose what might be most important to you. As Bessel Van der Kolk points out in *The Body Keeps the Score*, trauma doesn't go away; it will come out somehow, some way.

Consider athletes: no matter how good an athlete is, he or she maintains a relationship with a coach. This goes beyond the physical demands of their chosen sport. Nearly all have someone who helps them with the mental aspect of their game. Because of your military experience, you've been through more than elite athletes, so find someone who can help you process your experiences.

Talk with others who've walked a similar path. You may believe no one has had it as rough as you, but nothing could be further from the truth. Your experiences are unique, they are your own, but others who've served in the military also experienced similar overwhelming situations. Alcoholics Anonymous is a testament to this truth: there's healing when you can look at someone and understand each other without words. I believe this is why my father felt such a bond with other Marines.

Marine Families

For those who have a Marine in your life, my best advice is to extend as much grace as possible. I believe the goal should be understanding without judgment. Grace doesn't mean you have to accept their bad behavior. I don't know what I would have done with the experiences of my father. As noted earlier, you have no way of knowing how you would have responded to the situations your Marine faced.

Keep trying to talk with them. Based on what my father shared, and stories from other Marines, I understand why they want certain parts of their time in The Corps to become a distant memory. It must be incredibly painful to recount certain experiences. In my father's case, it took him decades before he began to open up, but that's the man I wanted and needed to know.

A close friend once described intimacy as *"into me see."* Take the first step and open yourself up. When you're transparent with someone, you give permission to the other person to do the same, and you communicate that they are in a safe place.

In a previous section, I mentioned counseling for Marines. If you see any signs of PTSD with your Marine, don't wait. Seek your own help immediately and encourage them to do the same. For example, Al Anon meetings help people who don't struggle with alcohol but have someone in their family who is alcoholic. Groups such as Al Anon connect you with people in similar situations and can help you understand how best to cope with a host of challenges.

If there's physical and/or mental abuse, quickly remove yourself from the situation. Don't brush it off as a one-time incident because it's never happened before. Don't simply accept an apology and move on hoping things change. Physical and/or mental abuse is a clear sign the person needs help. Your physical and emotional state are too important to roll the dice on whether things will change.

Remember, you don't need to wait years or decades before seeking help. The sooner you start, the better the chance for restoration for you and the Marine in your life.

Conscious Choices

As I noted when writing about separating the good from the bad, I have many traits that I learned from my father that have served me well in life. However, as I grew and reflected on our family history, I realized I made many conscious choices to set a different tone with my wife and daughter.

Knowing how much time spent with Dad meant to me, when my daughter Abigail came into the world, I committed to spend as much time as I could with her. One vivid memory that stands out was when she was about a year old. Jane asked if I wanted to go to the park with her and Abigail. I declined because I was feeling tired. As I stood looking out the kitchen window the thought hit me, *"I don't want Abigail to grow up wondering why I didn't go to the park or do other activities with her and Jane."* Before they got in the car I changed my mind, set aside my fatigue, and joined them. At that moment, it seemed like a small decision, but upon reflection, that choice helped establish a habit of spending as much time as I could with Abigail. I recounted that story many times to Abigail so when she got married, I ended my toast with a promise, *"I'll always go to the park with you."* That brought both of us to tears.

June 3, 2022, wedding day! Tyler, our new son-in-law, Abigail, Jane, and me.
Jo's wedding present was my father's Marine Corps sword.

Another example of my strong desire to have a better relationship with Abigail than I had with Dad occurred when a friend invited us to join Indian Princess, a YMCA group for fathers and daughters. Remembering how much I wanted to spend time with Dad, I took advantage of the program so Abigail would experience things I missed out on as a kid. Every month Abigail and I attended meetings with other dads and daughters, went to events like horseback riding or penny carnivals, and we did quite a bit of camping. One night, while reading in bed with Abigail, I asked her, "*What's the best thing about your life?*" She quickly replied, "*Indian Princess!*"

When it came to marriage, although Jane and I had some big obstacles to overcome early on, divorce was never an option. No one in Jane's extended family had been divorced at the time and she didn't want to be the first. Having lived through a bad divorce, the last thing I wanted to do was to put Abigail through something similar.

Throughout Jane's and my time together as a married couple, staying married was made easier by the fact that I deeply loved Jane and was willing to do whatever I needed to do to ensure that I would spend the rest of my life with her. I could list many other examples, but the few just mentioned illustrate my point. You're not captive to what's happened in the past. You can decide today to start making better choices.

Faith

Faith is an important part of my life. I hope that's evident from the number of Bible verses I've quoted throughout the book and some of the stories I've shared. I recognize that talking about matters of faith can be touchy, especially in today's society when people believe faith is a private matter. However, without faith I wouldn't be the person that I am. In all likelihood, without faith my marriage would have ended a long time ago, our beautiful daughter would not be with us, and my relationship with my father would not have been restored. Knowing that, wherever you stand on matters of faith, I hope you can understand why I want to share a bit more about my faith.

I've always had a sense that God was real. My earliest memories are filled with the assurance of God's presence and the peace that He was watching over me. Even in troubling times, I believed God would make things work out somehow.

Faith is like a muscle, the more you exercise it the stronger it gets. My faith was tested early on in our marriage. Like any marriage, Jane and I struggled, and I came to realize there was nothing I could do to change her, nor should I. The late Ruth Graham, wife of the late evangelist Billy Graham once said, *"It is my job to love and respect Billy. It's God's job to make him good."* My life changed radically when I cried out to God and said, *"Lord, I don't care what you do with Jane, things have to be right between me and You."* I think that's the moment when God said, *"I can work with you now!"*

During our lifetimes, we will all come up against people, situations, and issues we can't handle on our own. Despite our education, discipline, hard work, or anything else, there will be things that we cannot overcome on our own. People who finally surrender and join groups like Alcoholics Anonymous and Al Anon know this as well as anyone.

Contrary to what many people believe, faith is active. It's not sitting in a room, passively waiting for God to do what we cannot do on our own. Rather, actively trusting God gives us the strength, wisdom, and the resources we need to deal with whatever we're confronted with. Then, we act on what God reveals to us, and we walk through the doors He opens. Simon Peter only walked on water when he trusted Jesus Christ and got out of the boat. He trusted the Lord by taking a step of faith. That is the power of God working through us.

If I hadn't had faith, a wonderful church, and close friends who encouraged me, I don't know where I'd be right now. My faith compelled me to start having hard conversations with my father. Why do I write that? Apart from faith, I don't believe I would have had the strength of character to take that difficult step and ask the hard questions.

Faith is important for Marines, and not only for religious reasons. Serving in the military requires faith in the chain-of-command, faith in your band of brothers, and a belief that the mission will be successful. Despite their strength of character, Marines encounter life struggles that don't go the way they want. Surrender is not a word that resonates with Marines unless it's an enemy surrendering to them. It takes faith for a Marine to take a close look at himself and surrender to the truth; that is, to honestly admit he's said and done things that have contributed to his and his family's difficulties.

I've heard many stories from Marines that would make anyone carry anger, guilt, remorse, and a host of other emotions; emotions that don't vanish with the passage of time. Time does not heal all wounds. What I've seen during my lifetime is this; time tends to cement feelings unless they are properly dealt with.

Faith is the deep–seated conviction that things will work out for the best if we turn to God. Why? Because He promises, *"God causes all things to work together for good for those who love God and are called according to His purposes."* (Romans 8:28, NASB®)

Is faith scary? Yes, because in giving up control you don't know if, when, or how things will work out. God doesn't lay out His entire plan all at once for you, which means you walk in daily trust and not by sight. However, as you begin to see how God is directing your steps and working in other's lives, your faith will grow, and so will your joy.

James 1:2–4 tells us, *"Consider it all joy, my brethren, when you encounter various trials, knowing that the testing of your faith produces endurance. And let endurance have its perfect result, so that you may be perfect and complete, lacking in nothing."* (NASB®)

With deep trust in the love, wisdom, and goodness of God, no matter what you've encountered, one day you'll be able to say, *"Thank God, because were it not for my trials, I would not know Him as I do."*

Dad and Jo

Resources for Help

Reading our story may have triggered you or you may feel you or a loved one needs help. If that's the case, below are some resources you might want to explore.

- Alcoholics Anonymous: https://alcoholicsanonymous.com/
- Al-Anon: https://al-anon.org/
- Suicide & Crisis Lifeline: 988
- National Domestic Violence Hotline: 800-799-7233
- Substance Abuse & Mental Health Services Administration:
- https://www.samhsa.gov/find-help/national-helpline
- Veterans Affairs:
- https://www.va.gov/health-care/health-needs-conditions/mental-health/ptsd/
- Disabled American Veterans:
- https://www.dav.org/get-help-now/veteran-topics-resources/post-traumatic-stress-disorder-ptsd/
- Wounded Warrior Project: https://www.woundedwarriorproject.org/programs

Section 2:
Dad's Words

Being a Marine

U.S.M.C. Captain Brian F.X. Ahearn

The following is what my father wrote about his time in The United States Marine Corps. Except for some grammar corrections and explanations of abbreviations for non-Marine readers, it remains exactly as he penned it.

As you read through this section, you'll recognize some of the anecdotes. You've seen them before in previous sections of the book. I inserted excerpts of my dad's writing when I perceived they would add to the overall narrative. I lifted a story out of his journal when it helped you, the reader, better understand him or our family dynamics, specifically my relationship with him.

Still, I want to give you the unabridged version of my father's writings. Chopping up the text felt a little irreverent to me, even though their inclusion in the appropriate context adds to the reader's experience.

Out of respect for my dad and the countless Marines who share similar stories, I've included this section in its entirety, just as he wrote the entries so many years ago.

Below is what he wrote when he emailed me the document on June 13, 2011:

"Sometimes you do things for unknown reasons. I met a Marine some time ago who suffers from PTSD. He was in Nam a bit after me. He goes for therapy on a repetitive basis and part of the process is to face up to the experience and counselors suggest, among other things, to write about their experiences. Ironically, I have been doing the same for the past several years. I just thought I would do it. It is both good and bad to remember.

I keep the letter you sent for my 70th on my desk and read it occasionally. I was, and still am, heartened by your comments. There are many things that are still unexplained and perhaps the attached will answer some questions for you.

And perhaps it will raise even more questions. Maybe we can discuss it when we [sic: Dad and Jo] come to Ohio."

Prologue – Who is a Marine?

Brian F. X. Ahearn
U. S. Marine Corps, 1962–1969
Born April 22, 1941, Died September 14, 2020

"For over 221 years our Corps has done two things for this great Nation. We make Marines, and we win battles." – Gen. Charles C. Krulak, USMC (CMC), 5 May 1997

"The wonderful love of a beautiful maid,
The love of a staunch true man,
The love of a baby, unafraid,
Have existed since time began.
But the greatest of loves, The quintessence of love,
Even greater than that of a mother,
Is the tender, passionate, infinite love,
Of one drunken Marine for another.
Semper Fidelis"
—General Louis H. Wilson, Commandant of the Marine Corps Toast given at 203rd Marine Corps Birthday Ball, Camp Lejeune, N.C. 1978

"The Marines I have seen around the world have the cleanest bodies, the filthiest minds, the highest morale, and

the lowest morals of any group of animals I have ever seen. Thank God for the United States Marine Corps!" —Eleanor Roosevelt, First Lady of the United States, 1945

Foreword by Brian F.X. Ahearn

This is about what I most cherish, having been in The United States Marine Corps. Over the years, I have had many thoughts about my time in The Corps. Several years ago, I started to put them together resulting in this memoir. It reflects what I experienced. At sixty-nine, I don't remember all the names and places with great accuracy. The Marine Corps Command Chronicles put together at Texas Tech have been most helpful in putting events in a timely perspective.

History
Officer Candidate School

Before graduation from college, I was intending to go to law school but was talked into going into the U.S. Marine Corps by two college friends. This was done on the premise that we could have three more years of fun together. Two of the three never made it through Officer Candidate School (OCS).

OCS was a real trip. I had several friends who had been in the Corps, and they advised that I run all summer before OCS and get my hair cut shorter. I already had a crew cut. I went to Quantico with my two *"friends"* Barry and Jimmy. We had a government ticket from Penn Station to Quantico. Jimmy decided to exchange his meal tickets for beer. In D.C. we joined up with others heading to Quantico for OCS.

We arrived late in the day and my life has never been the same since. People did not speak to us; they YELLED CONSTANTLY.

One of our train mates had been ill informed on his departure for Quantico. He brought his golf clubs. While we stood in formation on the platform, each of his clubs was ceremoniously broken. What a terrible start for the day.

OCS was like a dream state for the first two weeks—everything in super speed—pee fast, run fast, eat fast. Garbage cans flying through the squad bay at ungodly hours. Slowly, some of us got the gist of what was going on. Keep your eyes straight ahead; listen to the Meritorious NCOs (non-commissioned officers); run; run fast and always say, *"Sir, yes Sir."*

Barry and Jim, my college pals, were having problems. I was in better shape and resigned myself to the daily routine. After about two weeks, we were given another more thorough physical. During the physical, Barry was found to have a curvature of the spine that excluded him from military duty. Barry was released. Now it was just Jim and me.

After about two months we were given leave and Jim and I met our wives in D.C. On the way back, Jim said he was getting out! I told him he couldn't without risking PI (Parris Island). Anyone dropped from OCS for other than physical reasons went to PI. He said he missed Cathy and couldn't go on. He was going to claim his bad knee was the problem. It worked and he was released about three weeks later. I was all alone, thinking, *"How the hell did I get here?"*

In October of 1962, the Cuban Missile Crisis was in full swing. We were on the parade field when our Platoon Sergeant called us to attention, had us face to face and pointed to trains loaded with tanks and artillery headed for South Florida. He said, *"We're going to war. You had better learn your stuff."* A scary time to say the least.

November was the loneliest time at Quantico, particularly Thanksgiving. I was used to large family gatherings and several days of fun with my brothers and sister. Not this year. I had a turkey sandwich at Diamond Lou's.

There are always people who you remember for the oddest reason. Candidate Wido; he was from somewhere in the South, maybe Mississippi. His name fit his body. He was 5-foot-7, 180 pounds, all muscle. One day on the parade field, SSgt. (Staff Sergeant) McGuire got on all our asses. He had us hold our M-14s straight out, shoulder level. He screamed all the time. Finally, out of exhaustion, most let the rifle down. Not Wido. SSgt. McGuire was getting angry, so he leaned on Wido's rifle and said, *"How's that Wido?"* Wido didn't say a word. McGuire leaned harder. When asked again if he would lower the weapon, Wido replied in the smoothest Southern drawl, *"Sir. Please get your f***ing hands off my weapon or I will stick it up the sergeant's a**, Sir."* The platoon was immediately dismissed.

Billy Dan Parker, better known as B.D., was a real western hero. B.D. was a bachelor at the time. He always complained that he needed "time off" to go to town. A lot of us were married, so we understood. B.D. was from Oklahoma. Most of us were 21 to 23 years old. Billy Dan was 29! To us, that was old. B.D. had been in the Corps as an enlisted man. He did his tour, got out, went to college and graduate school, got bored at 29 and decided to become an Officer. He had been through Parris Island, so he knew the ropes. They tried to break him, but he never bent. Old as he was, B.D. kept up with the best of them, talking all the while. B.D. did not have many teeth. He had bridges that would slide in and out as he spoke. He said he lost his teeth playing football. When he came back to Basic School, he was married! When asked why, he said, *"I got a pretty wife and a tax deduction."* He was married on New Year's Eve. No one could figure out where he found that gem in Oklahoma.

John Connor from Massachusetts was a member of our platoon. After commissioning, we became close as we went through Basic School. The wives banded together as most of the time we were at school or on maneuvers.

No account of OCS at Quantico would be complete without mentioning SSgt. McGuire, one of the platoon sergeants. Here was a man who could hyphenate any word and insert the word "F**k" without blinking an eye. "Un-f**king-believable," "Un-f**king-clumsy," etc.

We got used to it, but I remember that Dad and Mom came down for the commissioning ceremony. I suggested that my Dad meet me at the barracks. I was a little late. He was standing on the step. We hugged; he looked at me and said, "*Who is Sgt. McGuire?*" I said, "*He's our platoon sergeant.*" Dad, a highly educated man who rarely cursed said, "*I have never heard a man use F**k in so many different ways.*" *Dad was a quick study.*

Bushong, who would ever keep a last name like that? Poor Bushong! You could tell right away that he was not destined for "*Bars.*" He wasn't an attractive individual. He had a big nose, an elongated head, and a high voice. Every bad job was assigned to Bushong; just waiting for a mistake. The Sergeants got their way. They made Bushong 1st Sgt., responsible for the headcount. As expected, it was wrong and Mother McGuire jumped his butt immediately, "*You are f**king gone OOOO SONG! You don't belong in the Corps 'cause your head's shaped like a f**king piss-cutter.*" ("*Piss-cutter*" was the nickname given to the cover we wore). With those words, Bushong was gone. What a cruel man, that McGuire.

The difficulty of OCS was to blend in and not stand out. If you are too fast, they assign you to the rear; you carry those who "*fallout.*"

I never looked back on that except one time in Vietnam. It was my first firefight. Rounds cracking overhead. Thumps of grenades; the special sound of an AK-47. Was I afraid? No. I thought, *"Wait 'til I get back and get Jim and Barry."*

I was commissioned in Quantico, VA in December 1962 as a 2d Lt. (Lieutenant) From January to July 1963, I attended Officer's Basic School, also at Quantico, VA.

Officers Basic School

There are a lot of great memories at Basic School. At the time, Marines were in vogue. Gary Lockwood was filming a new TV series, *The Lieutenant*, at Basic School. We all hoped to get some face time. We got none at all.

There were overlapping classes at Basic School, so we got to meet officers we would see over the next three years. Several come to mind:

Major Ruthazer was the first officer I would have called a real a**hole. A fat little bulls**tter. For some unknown reason, the school put him in charge of guerrilla warfare training. People from New York knew more about that than he did.

After weeks of training, our assignment (as a group of six with me as team leader) was to find and infiltrate a *"rebel camp"* and attempt to capture the command post. We used our maps and decided that since it was a night exercise, most teams would make a beeline for the CP (command post). We decided to take the long route; way around the guards from SDT (special duty team). Sometime at O Dark Thirty, we found the camp; captured it and the major. He rebuked us for not following rules—i.e., coming straight ahead. I was polite, as usual, and said, *"Bulls**t"* and left. That resulted in my first reprimand in the Corps. Not my last!

A postscript to this episode is that Major Ruthazer became our Battalion Operations Officer while I was the Battalion Intelligence Officer with the 3d Battalion, 4th Marines in Vietnam. When he came on board, he noted that I was in his guerilla warfare class at Quantico and was very innovative. Three nights later he was on my butt, claiming I didn't coordinate some patrols so as to avoid ambushing our own guys. He did this in front of the assembled staff. He was wrong. Dave Usher, India CO (Commanding Officer), and I had coordinated, and Dave told him so in no uncertain terms. I think he even said he should get his fat butt out in the field every once in a while. From then on, Major Ruthazer and I were never close.

Back at Basic School

Several weeks later, we were all going through oral presentation training—How to Speak in Front of an Audience. Now! Come on! That's easy, particularly since they said we could pick the topic and it was only five minutes!

My topic—*"Hurry up and Wait."* This had to do with how we rush around only to wait and be given another, countermanding order. It was a great speech, but I ended up in the Captain's office for a second time.

The conclusion of Basic School was graduation and a formal Mess Night in dress whites (it was summer). As usual, it was the officers only and after drinking, to show our great skills, we ran the O-Course (obstacle course) at night. If you have ever been in Virginia, you will understand that there is red clay all over the place, including my dress whites.

While in Basic School, officers are asked to choose a Military Occupational Specialty, better known as an MOS. Originally, I had envisioned being a supply officer but was somehow talked into being an infantry officer. Captain Thorndike was our Company Commander. He pushed for me to choose infantry. His logic was that after the Marine Corps, I would have sufficient time to sit behind a desk. Now was the time to run around the "*boonies.*" So, I opted for 0302-Infantry. I was really surprised when I got my wish. CMC (Commandant of the Marine Corps) wasn't. It sounded like answering the call of Jim Mooney and Barry Coyle.

While at Basic School I qualified as "*Expert*" with the pistol and "*Sharpshooter*" with a rifle and had frostbite on my fingers from the beautiful weather in Virginia.

4th Marines Hawaii

I was elated when I received my MOS (Military Occupational Specialty) and was assigned to the 4th Marines at Kaneohe Bay, Hawaii as my first duty station. I believed then that I had died and gone to heaven. We arrived at Kaneohe in July 1963, and I was assigned to 2d Platoon, M Company (Co.), 3d Battalion, 4th Marines as a Platoon Commander.

The responsibilities of a Platoon Commander include training of the platoon for combat operations. Each platoon had 44 men. I was a platoon commander for about 18 months and was promoted to 1st Lt. and reassigned as Intelligence Officer (S-2) for the 3d Battalion. My duties included monitoring insurgent activities in the Far East and preparing the Battalion for possible deployment in the case of war.

The time in Hawaii was great. We met many great people, officers, and their families. Here are some of the real characters.

Dave Usher—he had been platoon commander for 2nd Platoon M Co. I took over that platoon, so Dave and I had a strong link.

He was a football player at Dartmouth and the prototype Marine. We both had young families, so we "family partied" many times. Occasionally, there would be a tsunami warning and those on base had to move to higher ground. Earlier in our tour at Kaneohe MCAS (Marine Corps Air Station), we lived in the town of Kaneohe, awaiting base housing. It was during those times that Dave and other families would come to our place and weather the tsunami. Actually, the tsunamis never came but provided great excuses to party.

Dave Fairbanks, Dick Camp, Ron Tamblin, John Mullen, and Don Burns were among the younger officers who always made Happy Hour.

Dave was Hawaiian born and lived in Honolulu. He was the Battalion S-1 (Admin Officer).

Dick Camp was a bachelor, as was Ron. They partied anytime they wanted to. As a group, our favorite stunt was to go to Happy Hour at Kaneohe Bay Officers Club and then someone would decide we needed to go to Honolulu-Pearl Harbor or Hickam because they had "free hamburgers." We would "shoot the Pali" – drive like crazy to get to the other side of the island before Happy Hour was over. I am surprised we survived.

Unofficially, Tamblin, Camp, Fairbanks, and I were known as MBO-March Bunch One. On occasion, we would designate one of us to be CINCPACMOB-1! -Commander-in-chief Pacific March Bunch One.

While we were in Hawaii, Hollywood was filming the movie, *In Harm's Way*, with John Wayne, Kirk Douglas and other notables. Ron Tamblin saw that they were looking for extras so we went to the Ilikai Hotel to see if we could get a part. No such luck, but our battalion was filmed making a beach landing and it was in the movie.

Years later I saw John Wayne and his wife at Fashion Island in Newport Beach, CA. I approached him and said I was a Marine who was in the movie, *In Harm's Way*, with him. He was gracious but probably thought I was crazy.

Dave and I liked the ocean. So, one day we decided to snorkel for lobster and other denizens of the deep. We decided Kailua Bay would be best. We were aware of a local shark—Charley—who never bothered anyone. We had some early luck and had a string of fish on a float behind us. That was a mistake that day. Charley came around and made ever tightening circles trying to find the fish. That forced Dave and I to swim toward a rock (lava) outcrop to avoid the shark. We cut the net line and made for the rocks. It looked easy until we got to the rocks. The three- to four-foot waves pressed us against the rocks, and we lost all our gear but got out of the water. Then we went to the base infirmary with pretty severe barnacle cuts. Tough day!

Ron Tamblin and Dave Fairbanks lucked out. They were senior and were due to rotate home and never made the trip to Nam.

Being a platoon commander was really great in Hawaii. The 2nd Platoon had some very good people. Sgt. Burl Wright was a Platoon Sgt. We became very close, and I learned a lot from him and other NCOs. SSgt. Talamoni was a Samoan. He knew a lot about running the platoon and had more recipes for C-Rations than anyone I knew.

I had more than one character in the 2nd Platoon. Cpl. (Corporal) O'Brien, a Bostonian, stands out for his numerous antics. He was a career Marine and had been up and down the rank ladder several times. Before I got base housing, we lived in the town of Kaneohe. Late one night I received a call from the MPS (Military Police) on base that Cpl. O'Brien was threatening to jump off a bridge. He claimed his mother was dead.

I rushed to the base and there he was perched on a rather low bridge over a stream, crying and drunker than a hoot owl. I asked him what was wrong. He said, "My mother's dead." Protocol in the Corps is to notify the CO in such instances and have him participate in breaking the news with the Chaplain. I had received no such call.

I asked Cpl. O'Brien how he knew, and he said it was because he hadn't gotten a letter from her in two months. I got him back to the barracks and we called his mother's home in Boston. Mom answered the phone. I explained the situation and she said, "If he wants a letter, he has to answer mine!" End of the crisis.

I can't stop without mentioning two others. Cpl. Starace was a squad leader from NY. A tough kid, to say the least. He was the kind of Marine you want by your side in the worst fight. He had a great comprehension of what to do in all situations. He just missed winning the Hawaii TO Squad competition. The corporal who did win in Hawaii eventually won the Marine Corps TO Squad competition.

Cpl. Hollowell was a huge black man and an excellent Marine. Somehow when we got to Nam, Hollowell decided that he could not kill his fellow man. He'd be in the Corps but carry a radio. That worked out fine until he was in his first major firefight. He helped his platoon get out of an ambush by charging, with a rifle, the VC (Vietcong), driving them into a riverbed where he proceeded to kill three, wound others, and break up the ambush. He received a Silver Star for his heroism. He saw the light!

Vietnam
Phu Bai

In late 1964 Viet Cong activities escalated and in March 1965 our entire regiment left for the Far East. We left Pearl

Harbor aboard many ships and sailed to the Marine base on Okinawa in the southern portion of the Sea of Japan. What a journey! As I recall it took about seven days to reach Okinawa. I actually enjoyed being aboard the ship. It was crowded but as an officer, I had run of the ship. I really liked being on deck and seeing the other ships and storms building on the horizon. The water was a deep purple blue. So clear that you could see the dolphins that often swam alongside the boat. Not everyone loved life aboard the ship. Many suffered terribly from sea sickness. I actually saw some Marines that had a green pallor. It's no surprise that Marines storm beaches. They are happy to be on land.

We remained in Okinawa for a little over a week while we prepared our ships and men for a trip to Vietnam. When we arrived at Camp Hansen, we had an opportunity to go to the O-Club (Officer's Club). I was surprised by the antics and behavior of the officers of a Battalion Landing Team (BLT) that was returning home after six months at sea. Women were allowed in the club, and it was truly wild. I thought we'd never be like that. Ha!

We left Okinawa in late March aboard the USS (United States Ship) Calvert-APA 32 for a five-day trip to Vietnam. During the trip it was necessary for our battalion staff to transfer to another ship for a pre-landing meeting. This necessitated that we be *"highlined"* from one ship to another while underway. Being highlined is fun if you like a scary ride. As the two ships move across the ocean, a line is shot from one ship to the other. Then a cable is stretched between the ships. To the cable they attach a basket and pull you from one ship to the other. It's like being in the world's largest slingshot!

In mid-April 1965 3d Battalion 4th Marines arrived off the coast of Vietnam near the city of Danang. We made one of those Marine landings across the beaches. No one shot at us.

I vividly remember Capt. Barnard, our Communications Officer, as we lined up, ready to "*go down the nets.*" It was early in the morning and hot. Capt. Barnard offered me a drink from his canteen. I took a swig of straight bourbon and almost choked in surprise.

We immediately moved north by helicopter to Phu Bai, south of the city of Hue. Being the S-2, I had all kinds of maps and as I do now, I had read books on the French involvement in Indochina in the 1950s. Phu Bai straddled Rt. (Route) 1; known as *The Street Without Joy* and the title of a book by Bernard Fall. Between us and Danang to the south, there were some 67 bridges, all of which were vital to make a land move to Danang. We were isolated, at least with regard to land reinforcements.

The recognition that our battalion was far from the main Marine forces in Danang was reinforced later by this excerpt from The Marines in Vietnam 1965: The Landing and the Buildup.

Although Admiral Sharp and the Joint Chiefs had already recommended approval of the Marine deployment to Phu Bai, one influential Marine general opposed this suggestion at the time. Lieutenant General Victor H. Krulak, then Commanding

General, Fleet Marine Force, Pacific (FMFPac) and perhaps the Marine Corps' leading theoretician on counterinsurgency, later commented:

Here is an example of where dollar economics wagged the tail of the military deployment. Phu Bai is as tactically indefensible as anyone could imagine. General Westmoreland was determined, however, that we should go there because of the existence of the 8th RRU (Remote Radio Unit). There was an investment of probably five million dollars in the unit. It was firmly locked to the Phu Bai plain and he was determined not to see it move. He was reinforced by the testimony of experts who said its location was particularly good from a 'technical' point of view. Whether or not this is true, and our own people strongly questioned it, he insisted that we go there despite the tremendous land barrier between Da Nang and Phu Bai, difficulty of providing logistical support, and the many better uses to which a Marine BLT (Battalion Leading Team) could have been put. I believe we would have been better off by far to have moved the 8th RRU to another place and to have kept our forces more concentrated. General Westmoreland felt differently, and Admiral Sharp was not prepared to override him.

Our battalion was responsible for securing Quang Tri Province from the demilitarized zone (DMZ) to the north of Danang. I was still in the Battalion S-2 and had responsibility for developing information on the VC (Vietcong) and assisting the rifle companies in developing strategies to engage the enemy. It was at Phu Bai that we had our first firefight—gun battle—with the VC.

We had several casualties among the Marines, but none were fatal. We killed several VC and captured about eight. It was my responsibility to interrogate these prisoners and obtain valuable information.

Within several weeks the VC increased their activities, particularly mortar attacks and sniper fire. We determined that there was a sizable enemy force in the area, so we developed a search and destroy operation. It was during this operation that two of my close friends were wounded.

Typical of government intervention in military activities, we were instructed not to shoot at anyone until they shot at us. That's like being in a gun fight and having to draw last!

Things were quiet for the first few weeks and then someone shot at us. Now we were playing real Marines. I had only seen dead people in funeral homes. Now I got to see what really happens when people die. Seeing dead VC was a little upsetting, but seeing a dead or wounded Marine was really tough. One of our first casualties was a platoon commander, John Stennick. He was shot in an ambush and had to be evacuated to Charlie Med in Danang. He recovered but his wounds sent him back to the states. In July, my good friend, Steve Kemple, 2d platoon commander for Mike Company, stepped on a booby-trapped grenade and received severe leg wounds. He too left Phu Bai for the states. Because of a shortage of officers, I took over his platoon for several weeks until a replacement arrived. On about the second night we were hit pretty hard from all sides. Bullets were everywhere. Ironically, my first thoughts were of Barry and Jim, now safely in the states and no prospect of the draft. I would kill them when I got home! In July we received some terrible news. Frank Reasoner was dead. Frank was a 1st Lt. with 3d Recon Battalion with us in Hawaii. He was ex-enlisted and one of the most gung-ho Marines I ever knew. Frank's unit was sent to Chu Lai in July to assist 2d Battalion 4th Marines. While on patrol his team was ambushed. With many wounded, Frank pulled several from the ambush and was mortally wounded while trying to rescue his radioman. Frank received the Medal of Honor for his heroism. I will never forget him. He epitomized The Corps. His citation is attached.

With few exceptions none of us had ever been in a combat situation. Two senior officers, Lt. Col. (Lieutenant Colonel) Woodrow Taylor and Maj. Watson, had seen action in Korea. Both were old war horses. Early on we had killed two VC in a night ambush. Division wanted body counts so Lt. Col. Taylor had the bodies brought to camp the way you would bring in a dead deer, on a pole. Gruesome!

After about three months, contacts increased and we were able to take some wounded VC captives. We needed information. One prisoner in particular was brought to the ARVN (Army of the Republic of Vietnam) HQ (Headquarters) for interrogation. The ARVN did not like any VC. The VC prisoner was gut shot and didn't have long to live. The ARVN decided to push him hard for information. Since I was the battalion S-2 (Intelligence Officer), I was present. They had dragged the VC out into the hot sun for interrogation. After a while, I couldn't take any more of the ARVN brutality and through an interpreter told the ARVN officer to stop. He ignored me and went on. I pulled my .45 and put it to his head [Addition: my father told me his words were, "Kick him again and I'll blow your f***ing head off!"]. He stopped and shortly after, the VC died [Addition: my father told me the man died in his arms under a tree]. I was verbally reprimanded by my CO who restated that we were guests of the Vietnamese. I always wondered if I would have shot him. I think I would have.

John Watson

I first met Maj. Watson when he was assigned as Executive Officer, 3d Battalion 4th Marines in Kaneohe Bay, Hawaii. The minute he arrived, things changed. Our battalion commander at the time, Lt. Col. Hicks, was perhaps the most ineffective leader I had ever served under in the Corps. On twenty-mile forced marches, he encouraged us by riding in his jeep along the line of marchers. I think they sent Watson to improve the level of training and readiness.

Watson was a big man, 6-foot-3, and about 260 lbs. He was nicknamed *The Bear*. That name was never used in his presence. One would think that he was overweight and unable to complete a PRT (Physical Readiness Test). Not true. He was as fit as the best of us.

Phu Bai 1965, Maj. J.E. Watson and Capt. Don Harmon, CO Arty

Major Watson had won the Navy Cross in Korea. Apparently, he had rallied some Marines and led a counterattack that secured a vital position. He was recommended for The Medal of Honor but received the Navy Cross. I came to know that he actually liked the thought of war. In training exercises and O Club meetings he would say things like, *"You'd better learn your stuff Mister. We're going to war."* He wanted a war and we wanted a complete tour in Hawaii.

When I look back on those days in Hawaii, I see that Major Watson was right. He was the motivator and Lt. Col. Hicks was the gladhander. After a Battalion Tactical Test, Lt. Col. Hicks was found unsatisfactory although each of the rifle companies was rated outstanding. In the course of the test, his orders were ignored—turn off the radio—and the company commanders took over.

Major Watson had one fault. He didn't like squeamish officers and made it well known. He actually picked on them as if to find a way to get rid of them. His favorite way of testing officers was to "*play the game.*" The game consisted of standing toe to toe with the Major and trading punches to the abdomen with the heel of the hand. His stomach was rock hard, and his punches would lift you off the ground. Everyone had to play the game at least once.

Other than these occasional lapses, the Major was there for every rank-and-file Marine. He had a great sense of humor. When he laughed, he looked like a happy Santa without a beard. Lt. Mullins and I became friendly with him and occasionally saw a lighter side.

The Major was restless in Kaneohe and when we mounted out for Okinawa, he was ecstatic. "*We're going to war,*" he would say continually. He was right this time. Within a month we landed at Danang and moved to Phu Bai, south of the city of Hue.

Our assignment at Phu Bai was to protect the Army's 8th Radio Relay Unit based at Phu Bai and protect the airfield adjacent to it. While we lived in tents and foxholes, the Army personnel had air-conditioned trailers and hot showers. Marines were not allowed in their compound except on official business, although senior officers such as Watson and Lt. Col. Woody could go any time. But only them, no other officers, or enlisted men.

I was reassigned as a Platoon Commander when one of our lieutenants was wounded and after several weeks in the bush, Major Watson took me into the Army compound. No one asked any questions until we entered one of the areas where we could shower. A fat Army captain questioned the Major's presence to which he replied, *"F*** you!"* with a lisp. We went into the shower anyway.

When Watson undressed, I noticed many old scars on his back and rear end. I asked him if that was from Korea. He said they were. Being bold, I asked, *"How did you get the scars on your a**?"*

Watson said that it happened in the fire fight in which he was awarded the Navy Cross. He was knocked unconscious in the initial assault by the Chinese. As they passed through the position, they bayoneted the wounded and dead. Watson was among them.

After being unconscious for a brief time, he came to, gathered the remaining Marines, and led a counterattack, driving the Chinese off the hill, securing an important position in the lines. In the process, he saved a number of lives.

At Phu Bai, Major Watson was relentless in his pursuit of excellence in every way. The new Battalion commander, Lt. Col. Taylor was also a *"salt"* and veteran of Korea. After several months, he could no longer overlook the Major's approach with certain officers and had Major Watson reassigned to Division HQ in Danang. By then many of us knew him better and accepted his antics as odd but bearable.

The Battalion Admin Officer told Mullins and me that the Major was leaving at first light on a chopper for

Danang. No one else knew. Mullins and I were there to say good luck and goodbye to a friend. As hard as he was, Major Watson had a tear in his eye. Not so much for the gesture of Mullins and myself as for the fact that a Division assignment put him further from his new war, for a while, at least.

Civic Action Programs

For the next six months we were involved in company sized operations and were working on *"winning the hearts and minds of the people."* Capt. John Mullen was our battalion CAP (Civic Action Program) officer.

I felt sorry for the Vietnamese. They were caught in a war of ideologies. If they supported the VC, we went after their villages. If they supported us, the VC went after their villages. All told, we were the good guys. I remember a time when we sent a small force into a village with doctors to treat the villagers. Later that night there was a real commotion in the village with shots and screaming. The next day a patrol was sent to investigate. The VC had heard about the medical mission and in retaliation had killed several villagers and had cut off the arm of a child who had been inoculated. We seem to get into wars we can't fight because of our preconceived notions of "the good."

I guess Washington was starting to get anxious as they started requiring us to make body counts of the VC dead. Gruesome work.

Phu Bai – For the Enjoyment of the Troops

We weren't in Phu Bai for more than a month when we learned that our area was part of a Vietnamese Military District-Dong Da. Technically, what the ARVN said was law. The Vietnamese colonel came to our CO and informed him he was building a Bar/Whorehouse on the edge of the airport! Obviously, the Chaplin objected, but to no avail. Vietnamese are very innovative. Within a week they had scavenged lumber and the siding was composed of flattened beer cans. They did quite a business and the battalion surgeon was kept busy curing NSU (Non-Specific Urethritis), a form of clap.

I returned later to the battalion staff as S-2. During this period, I flew a number of helicopter and O1E missions to locate enemy troops and direct artillery fire on troop concentrations. III MAF (Marine Amphibious Force) wanted us to closely recon the outer areas. I had done that in helicopters with HMM (Marine Medium Helicopter Squadron) 161 and we complained that it was scary because the choppers were slow and an easy target. So, they sent two Army O1Es to support us at Phu Bai. O1Es are very similar to a Piper Cub single-engine aircraft. Very maneuverable and capable of flying at slow speeds, making observation a bit easier.

I remember my first O1E flight with a black Army captain. I went to the strip with my gear including my flak jacket. When I got in the back seat, he said I had it on wrong, "Take it off and sit on it. It will save your balls." I really needed that word of encouragement.

The first flight was uneventful. The later ones had some inspiration for them. We spotted what was really a pink elephant on a trail. We moved in closer and saw that it was covered with red clay mud! It was probably being used as a pack animal by the VC. As we swooped lower, I started to see little bits of flapping cloth on the wings—rifle rounds! We left and called in arty.

Those pilots had guts, and I have great respect for them and the help they gave us.

Late in 1965, enemy activity increased significantly, requiring the input of more Marines into Vietnam. General Walt, commander of all Marines in Vietnam, asked for volunteers to staff newly arrived companies with combat experienced officers. Being a senior 1st Lt., I was eligible to become a Company Commander. I volunteered and was sent as CO A Company, 1st Battalion 1st Marines in the Danang area. Before departing Phu Bai, I was awarded the Navy Commendation medal with Combat V.

The Environment

Vietnam was a major change for the Fourth Marines who had been previously based at Kaneohe, Hawaii. Vietnam was brutally hot in the summer. Flak jackets were required but posed an awful burden in the heat that sometimes reached 100 degrees. Couple that with long patrols in the jungle with no breeze and it quickly sapped everyone's strength.

While the monsoons cooled the temperature, they brought constant rain and mud. The uniform of the season was a poncho. Outside the cities, there were no paved roads. The dirt quickly turned to calf depth mud and stayed that way until the rains stopped. Boots became caked with mud and seemed to weigh ten pounds each; equipment needed constant attention to remain serviceable. Many Marines came down with some form of trench foot due to being wet for so long.

Marines hadn't fought in a jungle climate for years. All the standard equipment was of little use. Jungle utilities, lightweight and quick drying in nature, were unavailable early on. Jungle boots, with their light weight and aerated sides, were as scarce as hen's teeth.

On the front lines, accommodations were spartan, at best. Home usually was a hole in the ground with a poncho for cover. The rations we were given were leftover C-rats from Korea, perhaps even WWII. We learned how to doctor up ham and lima beans into a palatable meal—just add lots of hot sauce.

Showers were a luxury. They usually consisted of 55-gallon drums filled with cold water. Enjoyable in the summer heat; freezing in the winter months. Every several weeks you had to be de-loused.

Movie Stars Visit the Frontlines

While at Phu Bai, we had visits from several Hollywood stars. On one occasion, I was asked to escort Robert Mitchum around our area. After the tour, he asked me if I'd like a cold beer. Of course! He had come into our camp through the

Army base, The 8 RRU. I told him I was not allowed in their O-Club. His reply, *"Come on."* When we entered the O-Club, his Army escort, a major from Saigon, said I was not allowed in. Mitchum's reply, *"Bulls***."* We had our beer.

Hugh O'Brien visited sometime later, and again I was slated to be the Marine escort officer. O'Brien was a Marine in WWII. We were driving in a Jeep toward one of the forward positions and O'Brien was using a tape recorder saying things like, *"We are now out in the VC areas..."* I corrected him but he kept at it the entire time.

Danang

In Danang, my company was assigned responsibility for patrolling south of the Danang airbase to prevent infiltration by the VC. A Company was composed of four platoons with a total of 144 men. At times we were reinforced with tanks and supported by artillery and air support. We would go out into the jungle for a week at a time and then return to Danang for a brief rest. During one of our long-range patrols, we were hit hard by a VC force, leaving us with several wounded. At one point, for fear of being overrun, it was necessary to call in close air support to push back the VC.

Air Cover

In 1966 I was reassigned to Danang as a Company Commander. Later I was reassigned as Battalion S-2-Intelligence because of my former experience. Due to some officer casualties, I was temporarily reassigned as a platoon commander attached to M ¾, my old outfit from Hawaii. M Company was led by Capt. John Keenan, my CO in Hawaii. M ¾ was headquartered on Hill 41, south of Danang.

My platoon was sent out on a long-range recon patrol. About two days out, we were hit by a large group of VC near a local village. The platoon regrouped in a cemetery for better cover. We were surrounded and needed air support quickly. I didn't have an ALO with the platoon and because of the proximity of the VC and their size, I called in an airstrike near our front lines. It was only partially effective, and I called in a second strike. That routed the VC, but it wounded two of my Marines. We were soon airlifted back to base camp.

After returning to base camp, there was an inquiry because of the wounded Marines. A fat a**ed Major from Danang came to Hill 41 and told my CO, Capt. Keenan, that he wanted to talk to the lieutenant who miscalled the airstrike. The Major was a jerk and started to really get on me, saying I didn't know my position and caused the mishap. After a few minutes, Capt. Keenan interjected, saying that I was one of his best officers and trained in airborne terrain appreciation. After about three minutes, he literally threw the Major off the hill, and we never heard from them again. I knew Keenan from Hawaii, where I served as one of his platoon commanders. He was responsible for me getting promoted to Battalion staff even as a relatively junior officer. A real Marine.

Even fire fights were not without their lighter moments. At that time Sgt. Burns was the Platoon Sergeant. I knew him from Hawaii. He was a massive black man with skin the color of polished coal. He had a great sense of humor. As we were attacked, we withdrew to a Vietnamese cemetery. These usually occupied a rise in the local terrain and were filled with pagoda-like structures. For protection, the platoon was set in a perimeter defense to repel an attack from any side. Sgt. Burns and I were in the middle of the formation. It was already nightfall, and we were planning our strategy for the night. It was hot and steamy, and we were both sweating like hogs. We were hunched over a map and I looked at Sgt. Burns and started laughing. Imagine his large round face, glistening with sweat and his eyes wide open. I said, "Shut your eyes, they look like headlights!" We got a real kick out of that despite the situation.

It seems that that one patrol caused more problems as another Danang officer visited our position to talk about breach of communications rules while in the field. When on a radio there was a specific protocol that needed to be followed. No real names etc. During our initial encounter on this patrol, we were warned of an enemy force by a Force Recon outpost situated in the nearby hills. When we first got hit, I identified myself as Mike 2 and the response was, "Is that you BFX?" Actually, he said Bravo Foxtrot X-ray. I replied, *"Yes, is that you O'Leary?"* It was O'Leary, a friend from Recon, and he got us out of trouble. He was the one who directed us to a more secure position before the firefight.

Movie Stars in Danang

As everyone knows, Bob Hope's USO (United Service Organizations) show visited troops in WWII, Korea, and now Vietnam. He was in Danang in December 1965. An officer friend said that his dad was Bob Hope's agent and that we could go backstage. I thought he was kidding. He led me to the back area and told a civilian his name and told him to tell Bob Hope. Minutes later, out comes Hope, who invites us backstage. If that wasn't enough, the female headliner was Joey Heatherton, a bombshell blonde. Imagine being in 'Nam for nearly nine months and the only *"round-eyes"* we had seen were nurses in C-Med (Charlie Medical). As Captain Barnard was fond of saying, *"Oh My."*

A Small World

While CO of Bravo 1/1, we were occasionally sent to the rear for R&R. After a particularly long period in the field and the loss of an officer, I was sent a replacement. I saw a Lt. approaching and when he got closer, it turned out to be Gene Papa, a classmate from Fairfield who had joined the Marines about a year after I did. Not a good environment to have friends, so I had him reassigned.

One of my platoon commanders was Charlie Wilhelm. Since we were in the rear, Charlie asked if he could go into Danang. Rather unusual for an officer, so I asked why. Charlie responded that a nurse he had met in Washington had herself transferred to

Danang Naval Hospital! I said that any woman who came that far deserved to see her Marine. So off Charlie went.

Air Force Resupply (Good Booze from Far away)

After 11 months in Nam, someone realized that I hadn't had the requisite R&R, so they packed me off to Hong Kong on one day's notice.

All I really wanted was a hot bath and rest in a clean bed. Immediately after arriving, I had my shower and lay down on the bed. Instantly, I was asleep. All of a sudden, I hear an AK-47 going off about 30 feet away. I rolled out of the bed, frantically looking for my .45 in my shoulder holster. I was in a cold sweat, no gun. Then I became fully awake and realized that I was in a hotel room. The noise (AK-47) was a jack hammer in the street. I was too tense to try to sleep so I showered again and went to the bar. I was still shaking when I struck up a conversation with an Air Force major. He too had been startled by the jackhammer, and we laughed about it. He was impressed that Marines lived all the time in the mud and rain and asked about the amenities. I said there were none. He asked if we had an O-Club, which we did, but it was in a small hooch with beer, no booze. He told me he would remedy that and asked for my name and unit in Danang. He said he flew resupply trips all along the coast of Vietnam and could get easy access to some gin. Never refuse a free gift.

About three weeks later, I got a call from the airfield in Danang that there was a large box there in my name. I sent our supply sergeant down to pick it up. What a surprise, a full case of Beefeaters Gin in the Imperial sized bottles. Did we ever have fun with Gin and Kool-Aid!

January 5, 1966

After several months as a company commander, I was reassigned to the battalion staff as S-2, Intelligence Officer. Shortly thereafter, we mounted a regimental size operation against a large force of VC and North Vietnamese regulars planning an attack on Danang. The operation was named Long Lance and targeted the VC forces along the Song Vu Gai River valley south of Danang. To move the regiment as quickly as possible, the 1st Air Cavalry loaned us their helicopters. I was in the second wave of choppers with the battalion command group. That was a random choice in order to confuse the enemy as to the flight containing the command group. The first flight had landed without incident. It appeared that the NVA regiment reported to be in the area had moved out.

As the second wave touched down, small arms fire raked the landing zone (LZ), followed by enemy mortar fire. I had not taken two steps from my chopper, and I was airborne on a mortar blast that landed several feet away. I never heard a thing. No blast. No sound of incoming fire. Just the sensation of flying through the air and an ache in my back.

Due to the heavy fire, downed choppers and wounded in the LZ (Landing Zone), the incoming Marines had to jump from the choppers in order to land.

Mangled bodies were strewn across the LZ. I thought to myself, "How can a leg be here without all the other parts?" Blood soaked the rice paddy and the cry, "Corpsman" came from every direction.

In less than a minute, the quiet rice paddy had been turned into a killing zone. The mortar and small arms fire became more intense, and the bull-whip crack of passing bullets laced the air. The dull whomp, whomp, of mortar fire continued as the NVA attempted to close down the LZ and strand those Marines who had already landed. More people died and confusion reigned.

The attack wounded our battalion commander and three other battalion officers who had to be evacuated out of the area. That left me, the S-4 and another officer and the battalion sergeant major to run the battalion until replacements arrived about four hours later. To be truthful, those were the most terrifying moments of my life.

Air controllers with the early group swiftly took over and directed air strikes on the enemy positions and soon the firing subsided as the Marines in the first wave moved toward the enemy positions. The lull on fire enabled the remnant of the command group to make its way toward the designated command post and begin to restore order and direct activities of the battalion. This was not a good way to start the day.

The first order of business was to replace the battalion commander. Within an hour, two choppers were on their way into the LZ. As they touched down, the mortar fire began with renewed intensity. The new arrivals, with one exception, buried themselves low in the paddy. The exception was a huge man, at least 6-foot-3, with a large head that made his hard hat look like half an eggshell. He moved quickly across the paddy, ignoring the mortar fire and moving the replacement troops into position.

The battalion Sgt. Major asked, *"Who is that crazy S-O-B?"*

"Major Watson," I replied. *"The Bear. I don't know who is worse off, us or the VC."*

Actually, I felt a little safer knowing that John Watson was on the hill, but I still hunkered down in the shallow ditch I called home.

Major Watson came up the hill, saw me and said with a broad smile, *"Nithe day, eh Lt. Ahearn!"* Major Watson had a slight lisp, but you never brought it to his attention. (See USMC Command Chronicles excerpt at the end of this).

By this time, it was April 1966, and I was due for rotation back to the United States. I left Vietnam in mid-April, flew to Okinawa, and then on to the States. I was awarded a bronze star in lieu of a second Navy Commendation medal. I was also promoted to Captain.

Returning to the United States

Upon returning to the States, I was assigned to the New York City Recruiting Station. I was a novelty being one of the first to return from Vietnam. I attended parties and gave talks at local colleges and schools. The best part of this duty was eating lunch at the 21 Club in NYC. It was owned by a gentleman named Krindler, who happened to have been a Marine in WWII and still a LtCol. in the reserves.

In December, I was officially released from active duty and served three more years in the inactive reserves. At the same time, I received a letter from HQ Marine Corps stating that if I returned to active duty I was in line for immediate promotion to Major. I felt I had done my part and declined.

Fast Forward 26 years

While watching news about the first war in Iraq, I saw that the Commanding General of the 1stMarDiv was Charles Wilhelm. I wrote a letter asking if he was the same Charlie from Danang who went to see his nurse friend. I soon received a reply that in fact he was that person and had been married to the nurse for 20+ years. [author's note: This is the same General Wilhem who wrote the foreword for this book.]

Fast forward to 1999

An article in The Ledger (Lakeland) stated that the commencement address speaker at Florida Southern was to be LtGen. Charles Wilhelm, who had recently been appointed as head of the SouthCom, General Wesley Clark's old billet. The same Charlie and, ironically, a graduate of Florida Southern. We got to talk for a while. It was great to reminisce.

Charlie stayed in the Corps and eventually became the second Marine officer to reach the rank of General (four stars) without being Commandant. Charlie was given this rank when he took command of General Clark's Southern Command.

Dublin 1980

It really is a small world, particularly for Marines. We moved to Dublin, Ohio in the late 70s. It was a small town then and when Breen [author's note: my nickname within the family growing up] played football, parents would gather after the game at someone's house for a few beers. Back then there weren't liquor licenses in Dublin. One evening we were at Katherine Hedley's. She was the mayor at the time, and her son played with Breen. We were just shooting the breeze when the Marines came up. I said I was a Marine and another guy at the party said he was also. We started comparing notes and found out we were in Danang at the same time! Not only that but he was in charge of an anti-missile site on hill 327. The same hill we guarded when we returned from long weeks in the field.

Leaving Vietnam Behind

Coping with PTSD

I t was as if I couldn't shake Vietnam. A good friend joined shortly after my return. Bob Burns was about my size, and he wanted to buy my uniforms. I sold him everything except my sword [author's note: the sword was Jo's wedding gift to Abigail and Tyler] and .45. Bob went to Vietnam as an infantry officer and was killed in the DMZ in 1968. Years later I met someone who served with him in Vietnam. He said that Bob was hit in the chest by a .50 caliber during a night attack. They found him in the morning, dead. His friend said he had a surprised look on his face. Ironically, Bob was platoon commander of 2d Platoon M ¾, the first platoon I commanded in the Corps. [author's note: Dad's brother Kevin was with Bob Burns the night before shipping out. Sitting at a bar, Bob told Kevin, "I got this eerie feeling I'm going to come home in a pine box."]

John Watson committed suicide in the early 70s. He had too many wars as did Bull Fisher, who shot himself at HQ Marine Corps in the same time frame.

Thoughts of Vietnam came back a short while ago when I participated in reading The Bible in 90 Days. While reading Psalms, I came to Psalm 23 (ESV®):

> "The Lord is my shepherd, I shall not want.
> He makes me lie down in green pastures;
> He leads me beside quiet waters.
> He restores my soul;
> He guides me in the paths of righteousness
> For His name's sake.
> Even though I walk through the valley of the shadow of death,
> I fear no evil, for You are with me;
> Your rod and Your staff, they comfort me.
> You prepare a table before me in the presence of my enemies;
> You have anointed my head with oil;
> My cup overflows.
> Surely goodness and lovingkindness will follow me all the days of my life,
> And I will [h]dwell in the house of the Lord forever."

Our chaplains always recited this Psalm before a big operation. Someone was on my side.

I still find Marine friendships the most rewarding of any, even if they were not from Vietnam. There is an invisible bond that joins us forever. If a Marine has a need, others will step in to help. It must be a carryover from being so close in such terrible times.

I often think about my two friends who talked me into joining the Marines. Most frequently when I was in Vietnam and someone was shooting at me. In retrospect, I believe they missed the opportunity of their lives.

Much has been said over the years about post-traumatic stress disorder (PTSD) and its impact on those who served in Vietnam and other wars. It is real and it is there every day. Some let it show all the time, while others bury it deep inside. In either case, it is there and always will be. The glory that we ascribe to the John Waynes of the world does not entail the pain that endures because of brothers lost.

Nothing I have ever done or ever will do can compare with serving in combat in The United States Marine Corps. At the time, I felt for the young kids of 18 and 19 years old. At 24, I then considered myself old. I was amazed at the everyday heroism and commitment of these young people. Older generations tend to look at the current generation and lament that they don't have the same resolve as they did. Not true! Just look at the young men and women who serve this country today. They are every bit as good as those of the past.

There is a saying *"Once a Marine, always a Marine."* It is true; Marines never say *"I was in the Marine Corps."* They say, *"I am a Marine."*

I am a Marine.

With all the antagonism surrounding Vietnam and the rejection of the men and women who so bravely served, I am reminded of a statement made by Teddy Roosevelt. It aptly fits those who served.

"Far better is it to dare mighty things, to win glorious triumphs, even though checkered by failure...than to rank with those poor spirits who neither enjoy nor suffer much, because they live in a gray twilight that knows neither victory nor defeat."

Resources

Texas Tech Website for USMC History in Vietnam
http://www.recordsofwar.com/vietnam/usmc/USMC_Rvn.htm

c. 5 January:

(1) The helilift commenced on schedule, but the heliborne elements were landed at (AT 795564) instead of the designated zone at (AT 806567).

(2) Company "C", in the first wave, landed without incident and moved to secure the landing zone to the north, south, and West. Within fifteen minutes of the initial landing, small arms and 60mm mortar fire was received from LAM PHUNG (?) (AT 800557). This fire on the landing zone continued through subsequent waves despite suppressive small arms fire delivered by Company "C", air strikes called in by Company "C" and 60mm mortar fire delivered by Company "D", after that company landed in the second wave. Eight members of the battalion command group, which also landed in the second wave, were hit with fragments from mortar rounds. The wounded, including the S-3, S-3 Liaison Officer, Operations Chief, Artillery Liaison Officer, and 81mm Mortar Platoon Commander, were evacuated by helicopter from the landing zone. Upon leaving the landing zone, Companies "C" and "D" initially moved west and south respectively, to position themselves for their assigned sweeps eastward.

(3) Company "C" discovered approximately 2500 pounds of rice in the vicinity of (AT 789564) and destroyed it in place at 051215H. At 051300H, the company moved into HA NHA (?) (AT 809554), and commenced destruction of another rice cache (approximately 1000 pounds). The rice was moved outside and set afire with a WP grenade. An unexpected wind caused the flames to spread, setting fire to several houses despite the efforts of Marines to control the fire. The sweep continued without significant enemy contact until 051700H, when Company "C" moved into night positions in the vicinity of HILL 52 (AT 788552). Two ambushes were established in this area. About 052300H, elements of Company "C" delivered small arms fire on a suspected VC attempt to ████████████ NG VU GIA about 100 meters South of the Company "C" position.

Frank Reasoner – Medal of Honor Citation

A reconnaissance patrol led by First Lieutenant Reasoner had penetrated heavily controlled enemy territory when it came under extremely heavy fire from an estimated 50 to 100 Viet Cong. Accompanying the advance party that consisted of five men, he deployed his men for an assault after the enemy opened fire from numerous concealed positions. Shouting encouragement and isolated from the main body, he organized a base of fire for an assault. Repeatedly exposing himself to the devastating attack, he skillfully provided covering fire, killing at least two Viet Cong, and effectively silencing an automatic weapons position in a valiant attempt to effect evacuation of a wounded man. As casualties began to mount, his radio operator was wounded and First Lieutenant Reasoner immediately moved to his side and tended his wounds. When the radio operator was hit a second time while attempting to reach a covered position, running to his aid through the grazing machine gun fire, Lieutenant Reasoner fell mortally wounded. His indomitable fighting spirit, valiant leadership, and unflinching devotion to duty provided the inspiration that was to enable the patrol to complete its mission without further casualties.

Frank Reasoner graduated from the US Military Academy at West Point, Class of 1962, the first USMA Marine Corps recipient of the Medal of Honor in Vietnam.

Command Structures
3d Battalion 4th Marines from Hawaii

USS Vancouver

USS Henrico

USS Union

CO LtCol. Jones (Evacuated with heart attack 24 April)

LtCol. Woodrow Taylor replaces LtCol. Jones

XO-Maj. John Watson

S-1

S-2 B.F.X. Ahearn Transferred to 1stMarines October 4

S-3-Capt James Conrado

S-4

CO-I Drost

CO-K Capt. Marino

CO-L Capt. Slater

CO-M- 1stLt. Deforrest

H&S CO-Capt. Seeburger

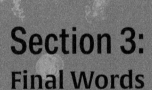

Section 3:
Final Words

*"For I consider that the sufferings of this present
time are not worthy to be compared with the glory
that is to be revealed to us."*
—Romans 8:18 (NASB®)

Brian Ahearn's Obituary

Appeared online 9/15/20.
Brian Francis Xavier Ahearn, Sr.

L AKELAND – Brian Francis Xavier Ahearn, Sr. passed away September 14, 2020. He was born in The Bronx, New York on April 22, 1941, to the late Cornelius and Helene Ahearn. Brian was the second of their seven children.

Brian was with Komatsu/Dresser for thirty years where he started with the company as comptroller and eventually became President of one of their divisions. After retirement Brian did some consulting but his happy place was when he was teaching financial management in the classroom at Southeastern and Florida Southern. He loved his fishing, never brought one home, just loved the catching. Brian is a Captain in the Marine Corps where he served in the Vietnam War. He loved the Corps, and he loved his country with a passion!

Brian attended Iona Preparatory School in New Rochelle, New York. He graduated from Fairfield University in Fairfield, CT, and received his Masters from Baruch School in New York.

Brian is preceded in death by his parents, Helene and Cornelius Ahearn, sister, Eileen Ahearn, brothers, Barry, Dennis, and Cornelius Ahearn, Jr.

Survivors include his wife Jo Ahearn, their Golden, Bella, daughter, Carey and husband Chris and grandson, Caleb of Glendale, AZ, son, Brian Ahearn, Jr. and wife Jane, and granddaughter Abigail of Westerville, OH, loving sister-in-law, Arlene Creasy of Gretna, VA, Nephew Chris Creasy and wife Stacie, Hood River, Oregon, Brothers Rory and his wife Victoria of Long Island, and Kevin and his wife Emma of Blue Ridge, GA.

Brian just celebrated his 38th wedding anniversary on 9/11 with wife Joanne Ahearn and precious Golden, Bella.

Memorial services, where Brian has been a member for 19 years, will be held on Saturday, 9/19/2020 at 2:00 pm at First Presbyterian Church of Lakeland, Florida. Masks are required at service. A reception will follow at The Club of Eaglebrooke.

In lieu of flowers donations can be made to Children's Ministries at First Presbyterian Church

Condolences may be sent to the family at: www.heathfuneralchapel.com

Abigail, me, Dad, and Jane on the rock at Candlewood Lake, Danbury, CT

My Eulogy of My Father

I woke up Wednesday morning wondering what I'd say today about my father, Brian Ahearn, Sr. There were tears in my eyes as I got out of bed. I sat down with a cup of coffee and immediately started to write in order to capture my unfiltered thoughts and emotions.

I speak for a living, but this will be the hardest message I've ever had to deliver. I ask that you be patient with me as I work through some raw emotions. I want to share a picture of my father, what we wrestled with, and the good place where we ultimately landed.

I wrote something recently and called it Fathers and Sons—It's Complicated. That summarized my relationship with my dad.

As a boy and young man, I admired my dad. When I was 10 or 11, I remember thinking, "Why doesn't he run for President?" I thought he was the smartest, toughest man in the world. As I reflect on that now, I know he was pretty darn close on both accounts. If you spent any time with him then you knew he was really smart, a sort of renaissance man because he seemed to know something about everything. However, I don't think you really knew the depth of his toughness.

My relationship went from admiration to extremely difficult when I turned 30. I was married, was growing, and changing a lot. I wanted to understand my dad more—the good and the bad—because I was becoming aware that his history shaped me. To say that he didn't want to go there would be an understatement. When I pressed him on matters of faith during a phone call he blew up, told me, "I don't care what you or anyone else says, I'm not a bad person," and hung up on me.

It was never my intention for him to feel that way, but everything changed in an instant and we started down a really rough road for a number of years. I was so angry I wanted to drive to his place and tear him limb from limb. If I'm honest, at 53 he would have kicked my butt up, down, and sideways because he was still that tough.

Sometime later we met at a restaurant to talk. He just couldn't understand why I wanted to delve into the past. I felt there were things that needed to be addressed so I could understand him better and myself. Things were said during dinner that didn't go away quickly.

You know my father served in the Marines during Vietnam, but you may not have known he wasn't drafted, he volunteered. He said the greatest experience of his life was being a Marine and leading men in combat. He was a warrior and I never saw him back down from anyone. I always felt like perhaps I didn't fully measure up to him because I didn't serve. That's part of the father son dynamic. Sons want to show their fathers they're better and ready to take the mantle. Most of all we want our fathers to be proud of us. Now that I'm older I realize fathers don't want to admit to themselves that they're no longer the biggest, the strongest, or most capable. That's the natural tension between fathers and sons.

As I reflect on this, if my dad were here right now, I'd tell him, "Dad, like you, I'm a warrior. I didn't fight for our country, I fought for something more important...I fought for you and me. I was willing to put up with the intensity of your anger and unwillingness to talk at times in order to have a closer, deeper relationship with you. I wanted to learn things that would help me understand you and help me be a better son, a better husband, and a better father."

The more I've learned about the trauma of war, the more I understand why my dad didn't want to rehash any of the past. He wanted to put everything behind him and just enjoy the moment.

He instilled such a strong sense of right and wrong in me that my wife called me a Boy Scout when we started dating. Although my dad knew the difference between right and wrong, having been raised Catholic, he struggled. He knew his Bible and I have no doubt he understood what Paul meant when he wrote, "The good that I want to do I don't do, and the bad that I don't want to do, I do. What's wrong with me?" (Romans 7:15 my paraphrase) My dad wrestled with certain parts of his past so much so that he once asked a friend, "Do you think I'm going to go to hell for what I've done?"

I know what was wrong with him and it's the same thing that's wrong with me, you, and every other person who ever walked this planet; it's the sin within us that causes the broken relationship with God.

Fortunately, our broken nature and bad choices are not the defining factor in God's eyes. In the Bible, King David is called "a man with a heart after God's own." David wrestled with his sin and so did my dad. But I think God looked at my father and said in his deepest place, his heart is after mine. I want to share a story that illustrates this.

When my dad finally started to open up, he told me when he was in Vietnam they'd captured a Viet Cong soldier. He was wounded and it was clear he was going to die. The South Vietnamese commanding officer kept kicking the dying man trying to get information out of him. My dad told me he couldn't take it any longer, so he pulled out his revolver, put it to the CO's head and said, "If you kick him again, I'll blow your head off." Then he sat with the man under a tree until he died. Nobody wants to relive moments like that, but those are the moments that define us because God is so clearly with us. I know He was with my dad at that very moment.

God's word says, while we were enemies, He sent Jesus to us, and He died for us. My dad put his military career and life on the line when it mattered most...for a man who was his enemy. That's the heart of God, no greater love, and I believe it was the core of my father. If you really knew my dad then you knew it wouldn't matter who needed help, he would jump into the fray because it was the right thing to do. As hard as it was for him to share that experience with me, that's the man I needed to know in order to understand him and myself better. That's the man I'm proud to call my father.

If he were here today this is what I'd want him to know—that whether or not he realized it, he had a heart after God's own. In the same way he volunteered to fight and endured unspeakable things in Vietnam, his willingness to fight again and endure emotional pain later in life helped me, my family, and countless others.

I hope by sharing this each of you got a glimpse of my dad that you didn't have before.

I'm sure God's already told him, "*Well done, you were Semper Fi, enter into the joy of your master.*" God rest his soul.

Where They Are Now

Brian and Jane Ahearn

Jane and I have been married for 35 years as of the writing of this book. We continue to live in Westerville, Ohio, in the same home we first looked at in 1990. After decades in the insurance industry, I stepped out on my own to speak and consult around the psychology of influence. The flexibility of being my own boss gave me the time necessary to work on this book. Jane and I celebrated the marriage of our daughter Abigail to Tyler in June 2022. It was the best day of my life...*so far!*

Carey Crabbs

My sister has lived in Arizona for more than 25 years with her husband Chris and their son Caleb. Following in the education line of the Ahearns, Carey has been an elementary school librarian for more than a dozen years. As she shared in her eulogy, she made peace with Dad. She and I have a wonderful relationship and had some bonding moments as we reflected on our past.

Ann Strausburg

My mother achieved quite a bit as a single woman, including earning an associate degree and buying a home in Columbus, Ohio. She's proud of those accomplishments as she should be! The years with my father took a toll on her because she never received an apology from Dad or any acknowledgement of the hurt he caused. Despite my father being gone for several years she's not found it within herself to forgive him. I hope she does someday because it will free her from much of the hurt and pain.

Jo Ahearn

My stepmom is doing well in Lakeland, Florida. Although she and Dad never had any children of their own, God blessed Jo with hundreds of kids as the head of children's ministry at First Presbyterian Church of Lakeland. Jane and I spend several weeks every year with her and have grown even closer since the passing of Dad.

About the Author

In addition to being raised by a Marine, Brian Ahearn is the founder of Influence PEOPLE, LLC. An international speaker, trainer, coach, and consultant, he helps clients apply the science of influence to ensure more professional success at the office and personal happiness at home.

Brian was personally trained by Robert Cialdini, Ph.D., the most cited living social psychologist on the planet when it comes to the science of ethical influence. Brian is one of only a dozen individuals in the world who currently holds the coveted Cialdini Method Certified Trainer designation and one of just a handful who've earned the Cialdini Pre-suasion Trainer designation.

Influence PEOPLE: Powerful Everyday Opportunities to Persuade that are Lasting and Ethical was Brian's first book. Not only was it an Amazon bestseller, but it was also named one of the Top 100 Influence Books of All Time by BookAuthority. Brian's second book, *Persuasive Selling for Relationship Driven Insurance Agents*, was an Amazon new release bestseller in several categories.

His third book, *The Influencer: Secrets to Success and Happiness*, is a business parable to show readers how ethical influence can help at work and home.

A LinkedIn Learning author, Brian's courses on applying influence in sales and coaching have been viewed by more than 500,000 people across the globe.

When Brian isn't influencing people, he enjoys reading, traveling, working out, good Scotch, and spending time with his wife Jane. Together Brian and Jane have one daughter, Abigail, who is an American Sign Language (ASL) interpreter. They live in Westerville, Ohio.

Looking for a speaker for your next event?
Connect with Brian on LinkedIn:
https://www.linkedin.com/in/brianfahearn/

Visit Brian's websites:
https://www.influencepeople.biz
https://www.BrianAhearn.biz

Email Brian at Brian.Ahearn@influencepeople.biz

A free ebook edition is available with the purchase of this book.

To claim your free ebook edition:

1. Visit MorganJamesBOGO.com
2. Sign your name CLEARLY in the space
3. Complete the form and submit a photo of the entire copyright page
4. You or your friend can download the ebook to your preferred device

Print & Digital Together Forever.

Snap a photo

Free ebook

Read anywhere

Printed in the USA
CPSIA information can be obtained
at www.ICGtesting.com
JSHW020039230524
63641JS00005B/291